Classic Country
CHRISTMAS

THIMBLEBERRIES®

Classic Country
CHRISTMAS

by
Lynette Jensen

*Decorating, Entertaining,
and Quilting Inspirations for Celebrating
Christmas All Through the House*

This book was designed, produced, and published by Landauer Books
A division of Landauer Corporation
12251 Maffitt Road, Cumming, Iowa 50061

President: Jeramy Lanigan Landauer
Vice President: Becky Johnston
Managing Editor: Marlene Hemberger Heuertz
Art Director: Laurel Albright
Creative Director: Margaret Sindelar
Photographers: Craig Anderson, Amy Cooper, and Dennis Kennedy
Photostyling: Lynette Jensen and Margaret Sindelar
Technical Writer: Sue Bahr
Illustrator: Stewart Cott
Technical Illustrator: Lisa Kirchoff

This book is printed on acid-free paper.

Printed in China 10 9 8 7 6 5 4 3 2

Library of Congress Cataloging-in-Publication Data available on request.

Foreword

For me, Christmas is a time for sharing meaningful holiday traditions with family and friends. During our 33 years of marriage, my husband, Neil, and I have added to our own fond childhood memories by combining those with many new traditions you'll find celebrated all through our home. The festive lights, ornaments, decorations, food, and gifts are gentle reminders that we are connected to those who have gone on before and those who follow after us. On the following pages, I'm delighted to share with you some of my favorite decorating ideas and holiday inspirations, with the hope that they will become as special to you as they are to me. With best wishes for your best Christmas ever…enjoy!

Lynette Jensen

Contents

Classic Country Christmas

Introduction

During the Christmas holidays, designer and teacher Lynette Jensen transforms her home into a magical winter wonderland filled with the spirit of the season—love, joy, and peace. For Lynette, the countdown to Christmas begins just after Thanksgiving Day, but she plans far ahead for organized holiday preparations that allow her plenty of time to thoroughly enjoy the festivities with family and friends. With careful planning and an emphasis on simplicity by using "what you already have on hand," Lynette's decorating, entertaining, and quilting inspirations for celebrating Christmas all through the house are a delight to one and all. As she shares them with you, discover for yourself how easy it is to experience the true joys of Christmas!

Back Porch

Living Room

Dining Room

Bedroom

Overview

Decorating for Christmas is something to anticipate far in advance of the holiday season. As you look forward to this very special season, Lynette Jensen shares her favorite decorating, entertaining, and quilting inspirations for celebrating Christmas all through the house. Lynette's desire is that from the moment guests first arrive, they are treated to Christmas joy outside and inside her home. She shows you how to fill room after room with meaningful holiday traditions that blend whites with brights for festive, unified decorating upstairs, downstairs, and from the front porch to the back porch. Even Lynette's enclosed, unheated back porch which is unused during the winter, gets trimmed in holiday style. Lynette fills it with favorite summer collectibles, dried hydrangeas from her garden, and a quilt made from her first quilt pattern for Thimbleberries®— the "Prairie Pines" quilt shown on the cover and at the upper left, opposite. The quilt is based on a traditional Laura Wheeler pattern and made using old-fashioned templates. However, the mixture of styles and deeper tones for the background represented everything Lynette loved about quilting, antiques, and country. At the urging of other quilters, she designed more patterns for Thimbleberries® that combine traditional quilt patterns with an appealing array of appliquéd vines, berries, and blossoms. The result is a charming blend of blocks and borders with soft touches of the country for a unique style reminiscent of America's more tranquil past.

On the following pages, you'll find chapters filled with recipes, ideas, and projects for surface design, home decor, woodpainting, stenciling, and fun with fabric for every room of your holiday house. Step-by-step how-tos, illustrations, and full-size patterns, along with a complete guide to materials and sources, provide a hands-on guide to creating it yourself. From decorating to entertaining, Lynette Jensen's signature classic country style offers you everything you need for creating your own best-ever Christmas holiday!

Welcome
SEASONS GREETINGS TO ONE AND ALL

The moment guests approach the house, I want to impart a warm,
"You are welcome," greeting. Thousands of tiny lights shining in the night sky
make our home a welcome sight for family and friends. It's almost as if it
is a scene from a Currier and Ives Christmas card joyously announcing
that "Christmas is coming…with seasons greetings to one and all!"

CHRISTMAS— NATURALLY!

In Minnesota, where winter usually comes early and leaves late, Lynette has discovered easy ways to decorate outdoors while keeping everything wind and weatherproof.

In the backyard, even the birds can enjoy the view overlooking the river. Lynette surrounds birdhouses (made from weathered boards still streaked with faded red paint) with green hydrangeas picked from her garden. Together, they dress up the patio in red and green holiday style.

In the front yard, an old iron-wheeled milk cart given to Lynette by her dad, has found a permanent resting place. Throughout the year she fills it with the season's bounty. For winter, Lynette first places a painted and stenciled wooden trunk (missing a lid) in the milk cart. Then she fills the trunk with tree tops, red-twigged dogwood, and dozens of twinkling lights.

NORTHERN LIGHTS

For Lynette and her husband Neil, the porch light is almost always on to welcome family and friends. The home they share in Hutchinson, Minnesota, is a haven of hospitality for guests and a place their grown children, Matt and Kerry, who visit frequently, still call "home." Cascading boughs of evergreens quickly transform the front porch into an arbor of wintertime welcome where a sturdy twig stand hosts a weathered birdhouse in the shape of a country church.

Lynette delights in finding new ways to use old things as evidenced by these "retired" but still useful sap buckets serving as luminaria. With cut-out designs on the side, each bucket is filled with sand and a small candle. Slender rounds of birch logs make it easy to display the sap buckets at varying heights.

WARM WINTER WELCOME

In early December a small forest suddenly springs up on the sidewalk leading to Lynette's stately two-story Colonial home. Lynette purchases several dozen of these tabletop-sized trees from the local nursery to give as gifts. After the annual Christmas party Lynette hosts at her home for the Thimbleberries® staff, departing guests each choose an ornament-topped tree as a special treat to enjoy at home. With dozens of Lynette's festive snowflake luminaria helping to light the way, who needs snow to make it feel like Christmas? To make the snowflake luminaria and ornaments, please turn the page.

FESTIVE LUMINARIA

Fabrics and Supplies
• Brown paper lunch bags, 5 x 10-1/2-inches

• Scraps for appliqué

• Paper-backed fusible web

• Sand

• Votive candles

Appliquéing the Luminaria

Step 1   Lay the fusible web over the appliqué shape. Trace the appliqué shape to the paper side of the fusible web. Cut roughly around the shape.

Step 2   Place coated side of the fusible web on the wrong side of the fabric chosen for the appliqué. Press with a hot, dry iron. Let cool, cut out on tracing lines and remove paper backing. Follow the manufacturer's directions if they differ from these.

Step 3   Position the appliqué shape on the paper bag. Press carefully in place with a hot, dry iron.

Completing the Luminaria

Step 1   Fill the bottom of each bag with about 3-inches of sand.

Step 2   Fold the top of each bag outward and make a crease along the top of the fold. This will keep the mouth of the bag open wide.

Step 3   Set the votive candles in the center of the sand, leaving the bag wide open. When the candles are lit, flickering luminaria offer a warm welcome along the front walk.

Luminaria Snowflake Pattern

Trace onto fusible web

STAR AND HEART ORNAMENTS

Fabrics and Supplies (for one ornament)

- 11-inch square of cotton fabric for front
- 2, 11-inch squares of black wool fabric for front edging and backing
- Perle cotton or embroidery floss (a contrasting color and black)
- Large button for decoration
- Paper-backed fusible web for appliqué
- Fiberfill for stuffing
- 1/3 yard of 3/4-inch-wide grosgrain ribbon for tree topper
- 1/2 yard of 1/4-inch-wide grosgrain ribbon for ornament

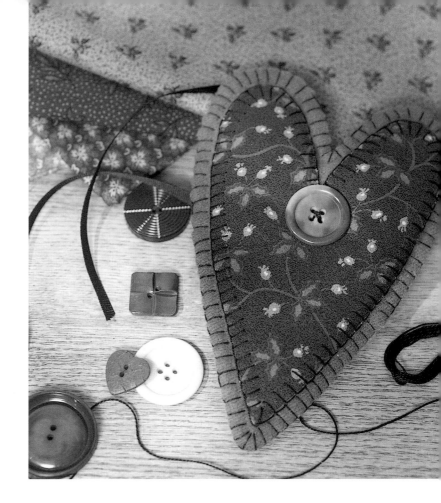

Step 1   Trace the shape (found on the following pages) onto the paper side of the fusible web. Press the shape to the wrong side of the fabric chosen for the tree topper/ornament. Cut out the shape directly on the traced outline. Peel off the paper backing.

Step 2   With a hot dry iron fuse the shape to one of the wool squares. Cut out, allowing 3/8-inch of the wool to extend beyond the appliqué edge.

Step 3   With contrasting Perle cotton, buttonhole-stitch the appliqué to the wool. Stem-stitch the lines on the star. See General Instructions for the Decorative Stitch diagrams.

Step 4   With wrong sides together, layer the appliquéd shape onto the second piece of wool. Using the appliquéd shape as a pattern, cut the second piece of wool to this size.

Step 5   With Perle cotton, buttonhole-stitch the raw edges of the 2 layers of wool together, leaving 2 inches open for stuffing the shape. Stop stitching, but do not tie off the thread at this point.

Step 6   Fill the shape sparingly with fiberfill to create a slight puff. Continue buttonhole stitching to finish.

Step 7   With a double strand of Perle cotton, stitch the large button to the shape as shown in the photograph. The threads should go all the way to the backside. Pull the threads tightly to nestle the button into the puffy shape and knot the threads.

Step 8   To finish the tree topper, fold the 12-inch length of 3/4-inch-wide grosgrain ribbon in half crosswise. Hand-stitch the folded edge to the center back of the tree topper; tie it to the tree.

Step 9   To finish the ornament, fold the 18-inch length of 1/4-inch-wide grosgrain ribbon in half crosswise. Hand-stitch the folded edge to the top of the ornament; tie with an over-hand knot.

21

**Heart
Topper
Pattern**

*Trace onto
fusible web*

**Star
Topper
Pattern**

*Trace onto
fusible web*

Decorations
ALL THROUGH THE HOUSE

It's easy to fill the house with old-fashioned holiday spirit using keepsakes and collectibles you already have—upstairs, downstairs, and all through the house. Choosing a theme for each room makes it even more fun! Here, the view from the French doors in the dining room is of the porch. Summer collectibles, dried hydrangeas, and the country-blue wardrobe swagged with pine cones, set the scene for a rustic collection of everything from stockings to snowshoes.

DECEMBER TREE PILLOW WITH RUFFLE

16-inches square

Fabrics and Supplies

Yardage is based on 42-inch wide fabric

- 1/4 yard BEIGE PRINT for background
- 1/4 yard GREEN PRINT for tree
- 1/3 yard RED PRINT for tree base and inner ruffle
- 5/8 yard TAN PRINT for border and pillow back
- 3/8 yard GREEN PLAID for outer ruffle
- 1/2 yard muslin for backing of pillow top
- Quilt batting, at least 18-inches square
- 16-inch pillow form
- A rotary cutter, mat, and wide clear plastic ruler with 1/8-inch markings

Pillow Top

Cutting

From BEIGE PRINT:

- Cut 2, 4-1/2 x 6-1/2-inch rectangles.
- Cut 2, 4-1/2-inch squares.
- Cut 2, 2-1/2-inch squares.
- Cut 2, 2-1/2 x 4-1/2-inch rectangles.

From GREEN PRINT:

- Cut 1, 4-1/2 x 8-1/2-inch rectangle.
- Cut 1, 4-1/2 x 12-1/2-inch rectangle.
- Cut 1, 2-1/2 x 12-1/2-inch rectangle.

From RED PRINT:

- Cut 1, 2-1/2 x 8-1/2-inch rectangle.

From TAN PRINT:

- Cut 2, 2-1/2 x 42-inch strips. From these strips cut:
  2, 2-1/2 x 12-1/2-inch border strips;
  2, 2-1/2 x 16-1/2-inch border strips.

Piecing

Step 1   Position a 4-1/2 x 6-1/2-inch BEIGE rectangle on the left-hand corner of the 4-1/2 x 8-1/2-inch GREEN rectangle. Draw a diagonal line on the BEIGE rectangle, and sew on the line. Trim the

In the living room, I always display a framed antique German die-cut Christmas greeting on the wall by the fireplace. The fabrics in the quilt and pillow were chosen to coordinate with it. For a fast decorating accent or Christmas gift, the rotary-cut and strip-pieced "December Tree" block on the pillow top works up quickly, even for beginners. The ruffle trim cut on the bias coordinates with the "Christmas Blossom" quilt. You'll find instructions for both projects here and on the following pages.

seam allowance to 1/4-inch, and press. Repeat this process on the right-hand corner of the GREEN rectangle.

Make 1

Step 2   Position the 4-1/2-inch BEIGE squares on the corners of the 4-1/2 x 12-1/2-inch GREEN rectangle. Draw a diagonal line on the BEIGE squares, and stitch on the line. Trim the seam allowance to 1/4-inch, and press.

Make 1

Step 3   Position the 2-1/2-inch BEIGE squares on the corners of the 2-1/2 x 12-1/2-inch GREEN rectangle. Draw a diagonal line on the BEIGE squares, and stitch on the line. Trim the seam allowance to 1/4-inch, and press.

Make 1

Step 4   Position the 2-1/2 x 4-1/2-inch BEIGE rectangles on the corners of the 2-1/2 x 8-1/2-inch RED rectangle. Draw a diagonal line on the BEIGE rectangles, and stitch on the line. Trim the seam allowance to 1/4-inch, and press.

Make 1

Step 5   Sew together the Step 1 through 4 units, and press. *At this point the tree block should measure 12-1/2-inches square.*

Step 6   Sew a 2-1/2 x 12-1/2-inch TAN border strip to the top and bottom of the tree block, and press. Sew a 2-1/2 x 16-1/2-inch TAN border strip to the sides of the tree block, and press.

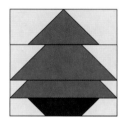

Putting It All Together

Step 1   Trim the muslin backing and batting so they are 2-inches larger than the pillow top dimensions.

Step 2   Layer the muslin backing, batting, and pillow top. Baste the layers together and quilt as desired.

Step 3   When quilting is complete, trim the excess backing and batting even with the pillow top.

Note: To prepare the pillow top before attaching the ruffle, Lynette suggests hand basting the edges of all 3 layers of the pillow top together. This will prevent the edge of the pillow top from rippling when you attach the ruffle.

Pillow Ruffle

Note: By sewing 2 different width fabrics together, you form the illusion of a double ruffle without all the additional bulk.

Cutting

From RED PRINT:
• Cut 4, 2-1/2 x 42-inch inner ruffle strips.

From GREEN PLAID:
• Cut enough 3-inch wide bias strips to measure 170-inches long for the outer ruffle strips.

Piecing and Attaching the Ruffle

Step 1   Diagonally piece together the 2-1/2-inch wide RED strips.

Step 2   Diagonally piece together the 3-inch wide GREEN PLAID strips.

Step 3   Sew the RED and GREEN PLAID strips together along a long edge, and press.

Step 4   With right sides facing, sew the short raw edges together with a diagonal seam to make a continuous ruffle strip. Trim the seam allowance to 1/4-inch, and press.

Step 5   Fold the strip in half lengthwise, wrong sides together, and press. Divide the ruffle strip into 4 equal segments, and mark the quarter points with safety pins.

Step 6 To gather the ruffle, position a heavyweight thread (or 2 strands of regular weight sewing thread) 1/4-inch from the raw edge of the folded ruffle strip.

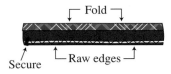

Note: You will need a length of thread 2 times the circumference of the pillow. Secure one end of the heavy thread by stitching across it. Then zigzag stitch over the thread all the way around the ruffle strip, taking care not to sew through the thread.

Step 7 With right sides together, pin the ruffle to the pillow top, matching the quarter points of the ruffle to the corners of the pillow. Pin in place.

Step 8 Gently pull the gathering stitches until the ruffle fits the pillow top, taking care to allow a little extra ruffle at each corner for a full look. Pin in place, and machine baste the ruffle to the pillow top, using a 1/4-inch seam allowance.

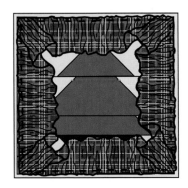

Pillow Back

Cutting

From TAN PRINT:
- Cut 2, 16-1/2 x 20-inch rectangles.

Assembling the Pillow Back

Step 1 With wrong sides together, fold the 16-1/2 x 20-inch TAN rectangles in half to form 2, 10 x 16-1/2-inch double-thick pillow back pieces.

Step 2 Overlap the 2 folded edges by about 4-inches so that the pillow back measures 16-1/2-inches square, and pin. Stitch around the entire pillow back to create a single pillow back.

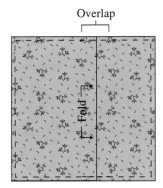

Step 3 With right sides together, layer the pillow back and the pillow top, and pin. The ruffle will be turned toward the center of the pillow at this time. Stitch around the outside edge, using a 3/8-inch seam allowance.

Step 4 Trim the pillow back and corner seam allowances if needed. Turn the pillow right side out and fluff up the ruffle. Insert the pillow form through the back opening.

CHRISTMAS BLOSSOM QUILT

43-inches square

Fabrics and Supplies

Yardage is based on 42-inch wide fabric

- 1/2 yard CREAM PRINT for pieced block
- 1/2 yard WHEAT PRINT for pieced block
- 1-1/8 yards RED PRINT for flower appliqués, lattice pieces, middle border, and corner squares
- 1/2 yard GREEN PRINT for stem appliqués, lattice post, inner border, and corner squares
- 1/8 yard BLACK PRINT for flower center appliqués
- 1 yard GREEN PLAID for outer border
- Freezer paper for flower petal appliqués
- 3-inch square lightweight cardboard for flower center appliqués
- 1/2 yard BLACK PRINT for binding
- 2-2/3 yards backing fabric
- Quilt batting, at least 47-inches square
- A rotary cutter, mat, and wide clear plastic ruler with 1/8-inch markings

The "Christmas Blossom" quilt is the perfect companion for a relaxing evening in a comfortable chair next to the fireplace in the living room. For the fabrics, choose deep reds and greens mixed with wheat and cream for a cheerful country holiday mix.

Pieced Blocks (Make 4)

Cutting

From CREAM PRINT:

- Cut 2, 3-1/2 x 42-inch strips.
  From these strips cut: 16, 3-1/2-inch squares.
- Cut 1, 6-1/2 x 42-inch strip.
  From this strip cut: 4, 6-1/2-inch squares.

From WHEAT PRINT:

- Cut 3, 3-1/2-inch x 42-inch strips.
  From these strips cut:
  16, 3-1/2 x 6-1/2-inch rectangles.

Piecing

Step 1   Sew 3-1/2 x 6-1/2-inch WHEAT rectangles to both sides of the 6-1/2-inch CREAM squares, and press.

Step 2   Sew 3-1/2-inch CREAM squares to both sides of the remaining 3-1/2 x 6-1/2-inch WHEAT rectangles, and press.

Step 3   Sew Step 2 units to both sides of the Step 1 units, and press. The blocks should measure 12-1/2-inches square.

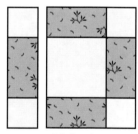

Make 4

Appliquéing the Pieced Blocks

Cutting

From GREEN PRINT:

- Cut 2, 1-3/8 x 42-inch strips.

Appliquéing the Stems

Step 1   Fold the GREEN strips in half lengthwise with wrong sides together and press. To keep the raw edges aligned, stitch a scant 1/4-inch away from the raw edges. Fold the strips in half again so the raw edges are hidden by the first folded edge, and press. Cut the strips into 8, 10-1/2-inch-long strips.

Tip: Lynette suggests laying the quilt block on a flat surface for pinning and basting the stems in place. This will help the stems stay nice and flat. Also, basting the stems makes appliquéing so much easier; no pins to catch your thread or prick your fingers.

Step 2 Position the GREEN strips on the quilt block, referring to the Quilt Diagram. Pin and baste the stems in place. Using matching thread, appliqué the stems to the blocks.

Using Freezer Paper Appliqué for Flower Petals

With this appliqué method, the freezer paper forms a base around which the fabric is shaped. The flower petals are appliquéd using this method. The freezer paper shapes can be reused.

Step 1 Lay the freezer paper, noncoated side up, over the petal shape. With a pencil, trace the petal several times and cut out the shapes.

Step 2 With a dry iron on the wool setting, press the coated side of the freezer paper shapes on the wrong side of the designated fabric. Allow 1/2-inch between each shape. You will need 64 petals for the pieced blocks.

Step 3 Cut out each appliqué shape a scant 1/4-inch beyond the freezer paper edge. Finger press the fabric seam allowance around the edge of the freezer paper.

Step 4 Lightly mark the midpoint on the sides of each 6-inch BEIGE square in the pieced blocks. Marking the squares in this way will help you position the tip of the flower petals.

Step 5 Referring to the Quilt Diagram, pin the petals to the quilt blocks. Position the 4 petals on each block center so that they are 1/8-inch in from the seam line. The petals will overlap a bit at the center, so trim away about 3/8-inch from the overlapping tips.

Step 6 Hand-appliqué the petals in place, using matching thread. When there is about 1/2-inch left to appliqué, remove the freezer paper. To do this, slide your needle into this opening to loosen the freezer paper from the fabric. Gently pull the freezer paper out. Finish stitching the appliqué in place.

Step 7 Appliqué the flower centers to the quilt block, referring to Cardboard Appliqué.

Using Cardboard Appliqué for Flower Centers

With this appliqué method, the cardboard forms a base around which the flower centers are shaped. This technique helps you create smooth, round circles.

Step 1 Make a cardboard template using the flower center shape.

Step 2 Position the template on the wrong side of the BLACK PRINT fabric. Trace 20 flower centers, leaving 3/4-inch between each shape. Remove the template and cut a scant 1/4-inch beyond the drawn line of each circle.

Step 3 Run gathering stitches halfway between the drawn line and the cut edge of each circle. The thread ends should be about 3-inches longer than needed.

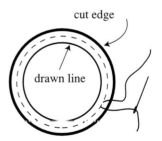

Step 4 Position the cardboard template on the wrong side of a fabric circle. Pull up the gathering stitches. Once the thread is tight, space the gathering evenly, and press. Knot the thread and remove the cardboard template. Repeat to make a total of 20 flower centers.

Step 5 With matching thread, appliqué the flower centers to the flowers.

Step 6 To press the complete appliqué, place the quilt block face down on a towel. Press gently with a dry iron. Pressing in this manner prevents the appliqué shapes from flattening out.

Quilt Center

Cutting

From RED PRINT:

- Cut 2, 2-1/2 x 42-inch strips.
  From these strips cut:
  4, 2-1/2 x 12-1/2-inch lattice pieces.

From GREEN PRINT:

- Cut 5, 2-1/2-inch squares. One square will be used for the center lattice post, the remaining squares will be used in the middle border as corner squares.

Assembling the Quilt Center

Step 1 Referring to the Quilt Diagram, sew appliquéd blocks to both sides of 2, 2-1/2 x 12-1/2-inch RED lattice pieces, and press.

Step 2 Sew 2-1/2 x 12-1/2-inch RED lattice pieces to both sides of the 2-1/2-inch GREEN lattice post, and press.

Step 3 Sew the Step 1 units to both sides of the lattice strip, and press.

Borders

Note: *The yardage given allows for the border strips to be cut on the crosswise grain. Diagonally piece the strips as needed.*

Cutting

From GREEN PRINT:

- Cut 4, 1-1/2 x 42-inch inner border strips.

From RED PRINT:

- Cut 4, 2-1/2 x 42-inch middle border strips.
- Cut 4, 6-inch corner squares.

From GREEN PLAID:

- Cut 4, 6 x 42-inch outer border strips.

Attaching the Borders

Step 1 For the inner border, measure the quilt from left to right through the middle to determine the length of the top and bottom borders. Cut 2, 1-1/2-inch wide GREEN strips to this length. Sew the borders to the quilt and press.

Step 2 Measure the quilt from top to bottom through the middle to determine the length of the side borders. Cut 2, 1-1/2-inch wide GREEN strips to this length. Sew the borders to the quilt, and press.

Step 3 For the middle border, measure the quilt as in Step 1 for the inner border. Cut 2, 2-1/2-inch wide RED strips to this length. Sew the borders to the top and bottom of the quilt, and press.

Step 4 Measure the quilt from top to bottom, not including the borders just added. Add 1/2-inch for seam allowances. Cut 2, 2-1/2-inch wide RED strips to this length. Sew 2-1/2-inch GREEN corner squares to both ends of the border strips. Sew the borders to the sides of the quilt, and press.

Step 5 For the outer border, measure the quilt as in Step 1 for the inner border. Cut 2, 6-inch wide GREEN PLAID strips to this length. Sew the borders to the top and bottom of the quilt, and press.

Step 6 Measure the quilt as in Step 4. Cut 2, 6-inch wide GREEN PLAID strips to this length. Sew 6-inch RED corner squares to both ends of the border strips. Sew the borders to the sides of the quilt, and press.

Putting It All Together

Step 1 Cut the 2-2/3 yard length of backing fabric in half crosswise to form 2, 1-1/3 yard lengths. Remove the selvages and sew the 2 lengths together, and press. Trim the backing and batting so they are 4-inches larger than the quilt top.

Step 2 Mark the quilt top for quilting. Layer the backing, batting, and quilt top. Baste these layers together and quilt.

Step 3 When the quilting is complete, hand baste the layers together a scant 1/4-inch from the raw edge. This hand basting keeps the layers from shifting and prevents puckers from forming when adding the binding. Trim excess batting and backing even with the edge of the quilt top.

Binding

Cutting

From BLACK PRINT:

- Cut 5, 2-3/4 x 42-inch strips.

Step 1 Diagonally piece the strips together. Fold the strip in half lengthwise, wrong sides together, and press.

Step 2 With raw edges of the binding and quilt top even, stitch with a 3/8-inch seam allowance.

Step 3 Miter binding at the corners. To do so, stop sewing 3/8-inch from the corner of the quilt. Flip the binding strip up and away from the quilt, then fold the binding down even with the raw edge of the quilt. Begin sewing at the upper edge. Miter all 4 corners in this manner.

Step 4 Bring the folded edge of the binding to the back of the quilt and hand sew the binding in place.

Flower Center

Trace 20

Petal

Trace 64 onto freezer paper

JUST IN PINE FOR CHRISTMAS

Quilted pine trees and stenciled pine boughs and pine cones complete the rustic theme Lynette chose for her porch decorating theme. (The "Prairie Pines" quilt is the first design Lynette offered as a Thimbleberries® pattern.)

And what could be easier than stuffing an old watering can with a "bouquet" of dried florals?

PAINTED PINES
Lamp Shade
Step 1 Dip the edge of a stiff sponge into stencil paint. Dab off excess paint. Use brown paint for stem; green paint for pine.

Step 2 Use edge of sponge to paint boughs. If sponge gets too full of paint, cut sponge to get a clean edge.

Step 3 To make berries, dip the very end of a small water-color brush in paint. Lightly touch lamp shade; repeat for each berry. Boughs and berries should vary in size.

Bench
Step 1 Using clear, acrylic stencil mylar, trace the designs, opposite. Cut stencils.

Step 2 Randomly stencil pine cones and boughs in clusters to fit bench.

Step 3 Use edge of sponge to add "snow" highlights. For berries see Step 3 above.

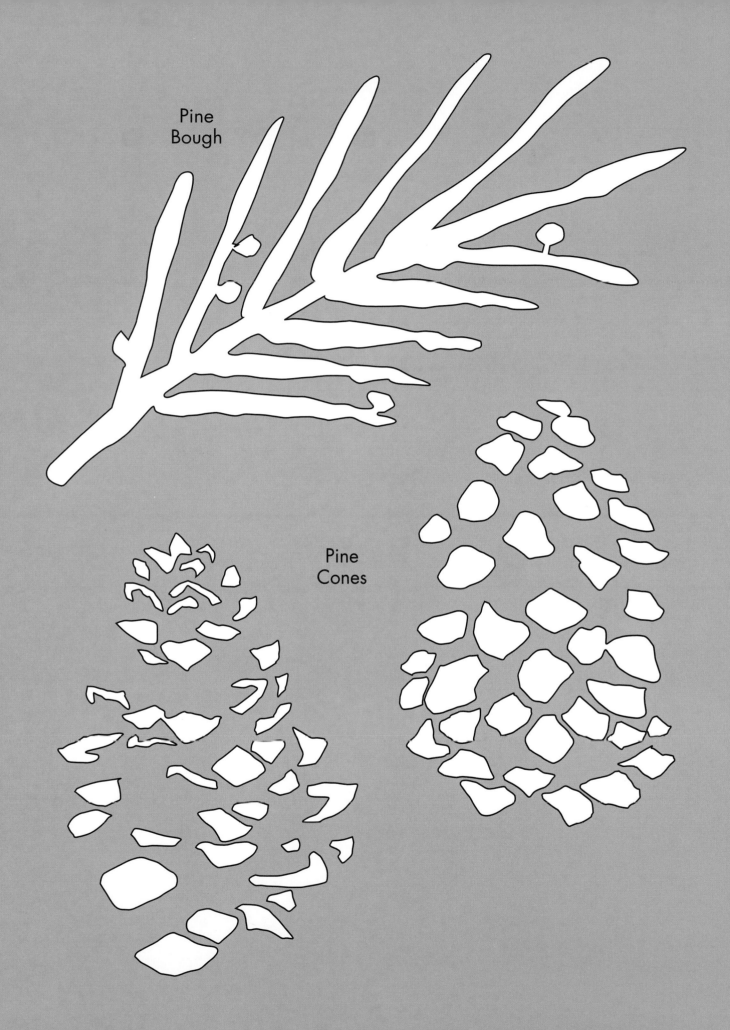

Pine
Bough

Pine
Cones

GINGERBREAD CANDLE HOLDERS

Just inside the back entrance, even the hallway is a welcome sight. Lynette fills the wall with a handsome pine cupboard lined with mixing bowls which she rearranges seasonally. At Christmastime her collection features Yelloware, green and caramel bowls brimming with artificial sugar-frosted fruit, pomegranates, and greens interspersed with homemade gingerbread houses and star cookie-cutter candle holders.

To make the candle holders, use the basic gingerbread recipe provided on the following page. (Vary the color of the gingerbread by substituting dark molasses for light molasses.)

Cut 3 star cookies from gingerbread dough for each candle holder. Cut 1 round cookie for base. Cut a hole from the center of each star cookie a bit larger than the diameter of the candle you are using. Bake on lightly greased cookie sheets at 375° for 10 minutes. Baking time may vary depending on thickness of cookies. Cool completely before assembling candle holders.

Layer star cookies on round cookie base and frost in place. Using a generous amount of frosting, place candle in base and hold upright until frosting is firm and candle stays upright. Hot-glue small berries and pine cones to decorate candle holder.

GINGERBREAD

1 cup shortening
1 cup granulated sugar
1 cup light (or dark) molasses
1 tablespoon vinegar
2 slightly beaten eggs
5 1/2 cups flour
1 teaspoon cinnamon
1 teaspoon ginger
1 teaspoon soda
1/2 teaspoon salt

Combine shortening, sugar, molasses and vinegar in a 2-quart saucepan. Bring slowly to a boil. Remove from heat, cool to room temperature. Add eggs to cooled mixture.

Mix flour, cinnamon, ginger, soda, and salt together and stir into the molasses mixture until dough is smooth and satiny. (At this point, dough is extremely soft, but it firms up when it is refrigerated.)

Divide into two portions. Wrap in plastic wrap and chill for at least two hours. (Can be refrigerated for several days if necessary.) Let stand at room temperature a few minutes until it is pliable enough to roll.

GINGERBREAD HOUSE

Roll cookie dough to 1/4" thickness. Cut out house shapes. Using a star cookie cutter, cut a star cookie for front of house. Bake on lightly greased cookie sheets at 375° for 10 minutes. Baking time may vary depending on thickness of cookies. Cool completely before assembling.

Make a very stiff frosting using powdered sugar and water. Frost edges of house sides and attach to house front and back. Prop house sections with canned goods until frosting has dried completely. Frost edges of one side of the house and place one roof section on that side of the house. Hold in place until frosting is dry enough so roof does not slide off house. When dry, frost edge of roof already on house and the remaining house edges, and place second roof section on house. Adding extra frosting to the eaves of the house makes it look like you've added a dusting of snow!

**Gingerbread
House
Pattern**

Side

**Gingerbread
House
Pattern**

Front and Back

**Gingerbread
House
Pattern**

Roof

HEARTFELT GARLAND

Fabrics and Supplies
- 1/4 yard red wool
- 1/4 yard black wool
- 1/8 yard gold wool
- 1/8 yard cream wool
- #8 black and gold Perle cotton
- 1 yard of 3/8-inch wide black ribbon

Assembling the ornament

Step 1   Cut the heart shapes out of red wool. Cut the stars out of gold wool. Cut the snowmen out of cream wool.

Step 2   Using black #8 Perle cotton, buttonhole-stitch the snowmen to the hearts. Stitch the snowman details. Refer to General Instructions for the Decorative Stitch diagrams.

Step 3   Buttonhole-stitch the stars to 5-inch squares of black wool, using black Perle cotton. Trim the black fabric so a 1/4-inch edging remains around each star. Using gold Perle cotton, buttonhole-stitch the black-edged stars to the hearts.

Step 4   Buttonhole-stitch the appliquéd hearts to 8-inch squares of black wool, using black Perle cotton.

Step 5   Trim the black fabric so a 3/8-inch edging remains around each heart. Cut out another black heart for the back of each appliquéd black heart. Using gold Perle cotton, buttonhole-stitch the appliquéd heart and the black backing heart together at the edges.

Step 6   Whipstitch the hearts together at the outer curves. Cut two 18-inch black ribbon lengths. Fold the two ribbons in half lengthwise and stitch them to the ends of the swag.

These quick-sew hearts work up fast for individual ornaments or gift tags (just use a fabric pen to add names to the center of the star or snowman). For a centerpiece of connected hearts, alternate motifs and whipstitch the hearts together at the outer curves.

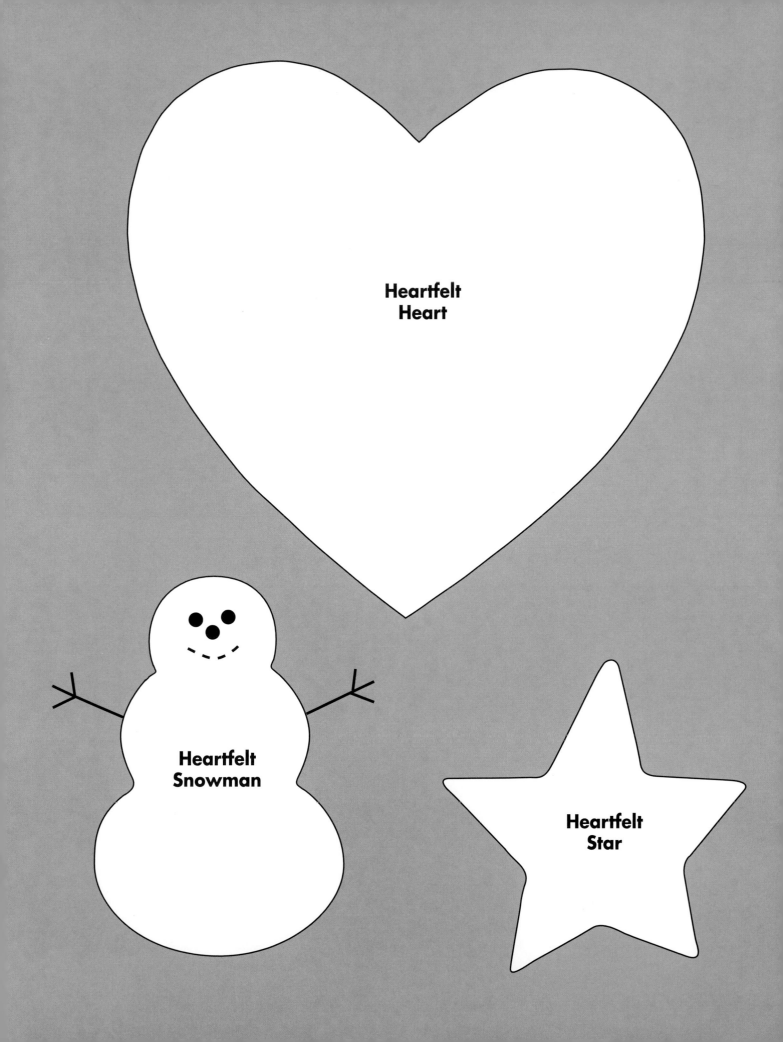

Heartfelt Heart

Heartfelt Snowman

Heartfelt Star

SNOW FUN CANISTERS

Supplies
- 9-inch diameter blue enamel canister
- Acrylic paints: white, gold, black and brown
- Mylar to make stencils
- X-acto™ knife
- Stencil brush
- Florist foam base (optional)
- Sprigs of greens

Cutting the stencil
Trace the stencil pattern onto the Mylar with a fine-tipped permanent marker. Lay the traced Mylar on a very hard flat surface such as glass. Cut the shapes out using the X-acto™ knife. The arms and nose are cut as one unit.

Stenciling the can
Position a snowman under each handle, at front and back center, and one between each of those for a total of 8 snowmen.

Step 1   Tape the snowman stencil to the outer pot.

Step 2   Using a small amount of paint, dip your stencil brush into the paint. Wipe off excess paint onto a paper towel, the brush should be almost dry.

Step 3   Tap or swirl the brush in the openings of the stencil. Move the stencil to the next snowman position to be stenciled. Repeat stencil painting for the remaining snowmen.

Step 4   The snow-bank background is dabbed on between the snowmen.

Step 5   The arms and nose are both painted with the brown paint. They are done as one unit for every other snowman. The alternating snowmen noses are stenciled, then the stencil is turned upside down and the arms are stenciled. Refer to photograph.

With the addition of simple snowmen stencils, the outside of the canister becomes a planter and the inside strainer, shown above, filled with candles for a glowing luminaria.

Step 6   The dots for the eyes, mouth, and buttons are done with black paint. Dip the tip of a pencil, wooden skewer, or the wooden end of a very thin paint brush into the paint and *dot* on features.

Step 7   A gold star is stenciled on either side of the front and back center snowman.

Step 8   The strainer is stenciled with 4 snowmen which are positioned between the holes. The arms and nose are stenciled as one unit. Repeat Step 4 for snow-banks and Step 6 for dots. With gold paint, stars are stenciled on the holes between each snowman.

Step 9   The lid can be stenciled with stars.

Step 10 Florist foam base is placed inside the containers to give support to the arrangement. Position sprigs of greens.

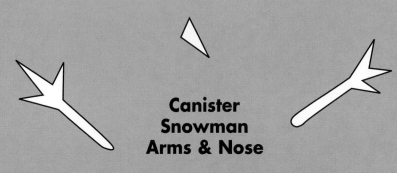

**Canister
Snowman
Arms & Nose**

Cut as one unit

**Canister
Star**

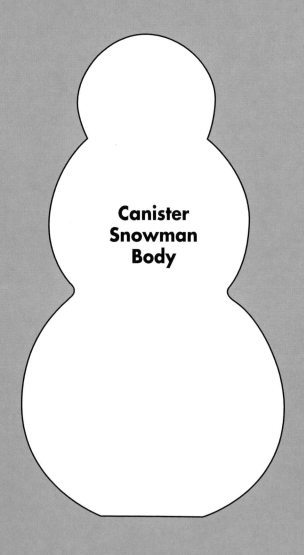

**Canister
Snowman
Body**

SEASONS GREETINGS

For the family room, Lynette's decorating theme includes an old apple box with its original stenciled greeting still intact, and Santas of all shapes and sizes. From her collection of antiques, every year she brings out an unusually-decorated cone-shaped tree stand (which actually holds nearly a gallon of water), secures a small tree in place, and displays the tree and stand on an old sled commonly used for hauling wood for the kitchen cook stove.

On the opposite side of the room, the cabinet for the television is topped with some of Lynette's favorite Santa images carved from wood. Three Santas are from a quilter in Salina, Kansas, whose husband hand-carved and painted them to match the quilts his wife had made using patterns and fabrics from Thimbleberries®.

Gifts
TO MAKE IN THE TWINKLING OF AN EYE

*Gifts are an integral part of the holiday tradition, representing the
mystery and excitement we anticipate for months in advance of Christmas Day.
A beautifully-wrapped gift offers no clue as to its contents, but it does say a lot
about the giver, right down to the gift tag. Each year I try to find new and
creative ways to make the presentation as interesting as the gift itself!*

GIFTS TO GO

Each year, Lynette's gifts for the staff Christmas party are uniquely wrapped and placed on the steps near the front foyer. She loves the visual impact and the excitement when guests arrive at the front door. For the boots that top each wrapped gift, Lynette paints papier-mâché boots red, adds diamond dust with Modge Podge® on the cuff, and fills them with pine, holly, and peppermint candy canes. Name tags are created using vintage Christmas stickers.

The Santa theme is established early on by an N.C. Wyeth print that is brought out on Thanksgiving evening when Lynette's holiday decorating begins in earnest. By Christmas morning when guests and family gather in the living room, they are treated to a tree trimmed with glass balls, gold stars, snowflakes, and tassels. It is surrounded by gifts wrapped in Santa paper along with milk and ginger cookies frosted with stars applied freehand with a knife.

To complete the theme, vintage Santa post cards are mounted on a rectangle of black mat board and "framed" by elegant gold-textured mats.

For gift-giving, Lynette suggests simply substituting favorite Santa images from contemporary Christmas cards saved from year to year.

CHRISTMAS SNOW WALL QUILT

24 x 32-inches

Fabrics and Supplies

Yardage is based on 42-inch wide fabric

- 5/8 yard BEIGE PRINT for background and checkerboard
- 1/4 yard BLACK PRINT for checkerboard
- 7 x 10-inch rectangle GREEN PRINT #1 for large tree appliqué
- 9 x 11-inch rectangle GREEN PRINT #2 for small tree appliqué
- 12-inch square CREAM PRINT for snowflake appliqués
- 1/3 yard RED PRINT for inner border
- 3/8 yard BROWN PRINT for outer border
- 1/2 yard Paper-backed fusible web
- 1/3 yard BLACK PRINT for binding
- 1 yard backing fabric
- Quilt batting, at least 28 x 36-inches
- #8 black Perle cotton
- A rotary cutter, mat, and wide clear plastic ruler with 1/8-inch markings

Cutting

From BEIGE PRINT:
- Cut 1, 14-1/2 x 16-1/2-inch rectangle for background.
- Cut 1, 2-1/2 x 42-inch strip for checkerboard.

From BLACK PRINT:
- Cut 1, 2-1/2 x 42-inch strip. From this strip cut one 2-1/2-inch square. The remainder of the strip will be used for checkerboard strip piecing.

From RED PRINT:
- Cut 2, 2-1/2 x 14-1/2-inch strips and 2, 2-1/2 x 26-1/2-inch strips for inner border.

From BROWN PRINT:
- Cut 3, 3-1/2 x 42-inch strips for outer border. Diagonally piece the strips as needed.

A small wall quilt is always a "must" on my Christmas gift list. I design using simple appliqué shapes and rotary-cut strip piecing so that I can quickly make several at a time. It's fun to share Minnesota snowflakes with friends who live in warmer regions.

Assembling the Checkerboard

Step 1   Aligning long edges, sew the 2-1/2 x 42-inch BEIGE and BLACK strips together, and press. Refer to General Instructions for Hints and Helps for Pressing Strip Sets. Cut the strip set into segments.

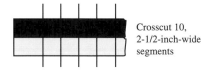

Crosscut 10, 2-1/2-inch-wide segments

Step 2   Sew 7, Step 1 segments together, side to side, and press.

Step 3 Sew 3 segments together, end to end, and press. Add a 2-1/2-inch BLACK square to the end, and press.

Step 4 Sew the Step 3 strip to the bottom of the Step 2 strip, and press. At this point the checkerboard unit should measure 6-1/2 x 14-1/2-inches.

Step 5 Sew the 14-1/2 x 16-1/2-inch BEIGE rectangle to the top of the checkerboard, and press.

Inner Border

Step 1 Sew the 2-1/2 x 14-1/2-inch RED strips to the top and bottom of the quilt, and press.

Step 2 Sew the 2-1/2 x 26-1/2-inch RED strips to the sides of the quilt, and press.

Step 3 Stay-stitch a scant 1/4-inch from the outside edges to stabilize the quilt before adding the appliqué.

Fusible Appliqué

Step 1 Read and follow the manufacturer's directions for the fusible web.

Step 2 Trace the appliqué designs (found on the following pages) onto the paper side of the fusible web, leaving 1/2-inch between each shape. Cut around each traced shape, roughly 1/4-inch outside of the traced line.

Step 3 Following manufacturer's directions, fuse each shape to the wrong side of the designated appliqué fabrics. Cut out each shape on the drawn line and peel away the backing paper.

Step 4 Arrange the appliqué shapes on the quilt top, referring to the quilt diagram. The trees should be placed 1/4-inch above the checkerboard. The center snowflake should extend 1-inch into the top inner border. The side snowflakes should be 2-1/2-inches from the top of the BEIGE background piece and should extend

3/4-inch into the side inner borders. When everything is in position, fuse in place.

Step 5 With black Perle cotton, buttonhole-stitch around the appliqué shapes.

Outer Border

Step 1 Measure the quilt from left to right, through the middle, to determine the length of the top and bottom borders. Cut 2, 3-1/2-inch wide BROWN strips to this measurement. Sew the borders to the quilt, and press.

Step 2 Measure the quilt from top to bottom, through the middle, to determine the length of the side borders. Cut 2, 3-1/2-inch wide BROWN strips to this measurement. Sew the borders to the quilt, and press.

Putting It All Together

Step 1 Trim the backing and batting so they are 4-inches larger than the quilt top.

Step 2 Mark the quilt top for quilting. Layer the backing, batting, and quilt top. Baste the 3 layers together and quilt.

Step 3 When the quilting is complete, hand-baste the 3 layers together a scant 1/4-inch from the raw edge. This hand basting keeps the layers from shifting and prevents puckers from forming when adding the binding. Trim excess batting and backing even with the edge of the quilt top.

Binding

Cutting

From BLACK PRINT:

- Cut 4, 2-3/4 x 42-inch strips.

Step 1 Diagonally piece the strips together. Fold the strip in half lengthwise, wrong sides together, and press.

Step 2 With raw edges of the binding and quilt top even, stitch with a 3/8-inch seam allowance.

Step 3 Miter binding at the corners. To do so, stop sewing 3/8-inch from the corner of the quilt. Flip the binding strip up and away from the quilt, then fold the binding down even with the raw edge of the quilt. Begin sewing at the upper edge. Miter all 4 corners in this manner.

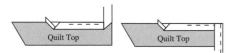

Step 4 Bring the folded edge of the binding to the back of the quilt and hand-sew the binding in place.

Christmas Snow Small Tree

Trace 2 onto fusible web

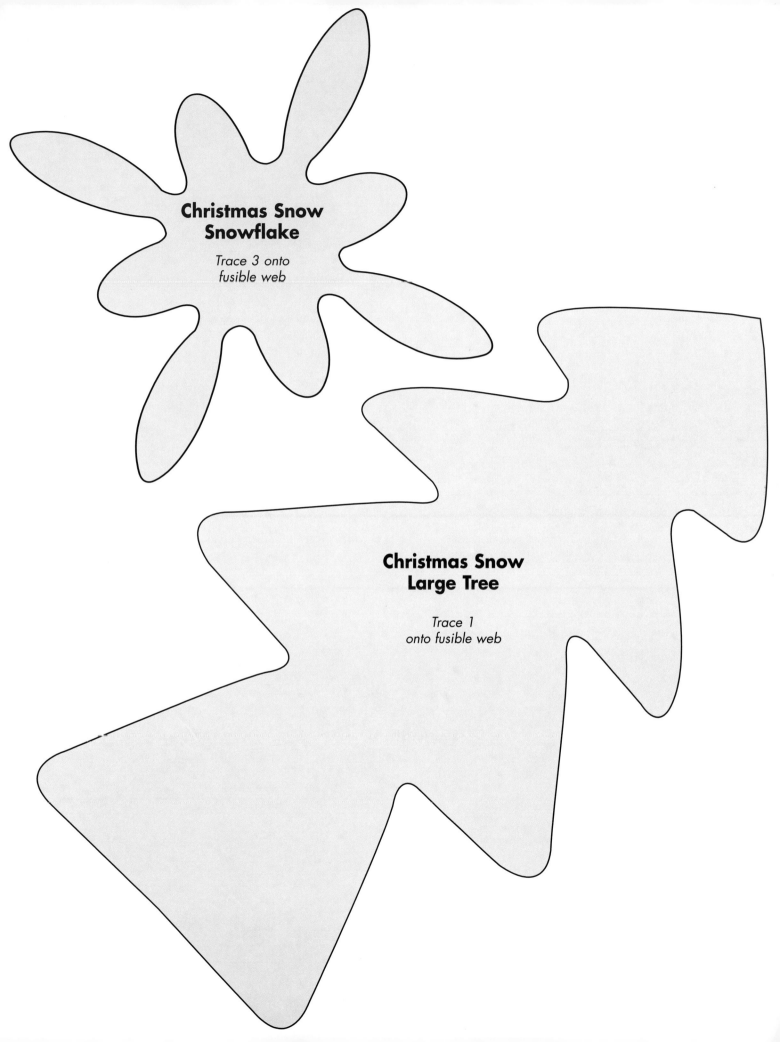

**Christmas Snow
Snowflake**

*Trace 3 onto
fusible web*

**Christmas Snow
Large Tree**

*Trace 1
onto fusible web*

MITTEN TRIMS

Fabrics and Supplies

- A pair of mittens
- 5-inch squares of green, white, and gold wool or felt for appliqués
- Assorted colors of embroidery floss or #8 Perle cotton
- 1/4 yard fusible web with paper-backing for appliqués
- Rit® dye (optional)

Step 1 Position the fusible web (paper side up) over the appliqué shapes, leaving 1/2-inch between each tracing. Cut out the pieces roughly 1/4-inch outside of the traced lines.

Step 2 Press the fusible web shapes onto the back of the fabrics for the appliqués. Cut out the shapes on the drawn lines. Peel the paper from the fabric.

Step 3 Position the appliqués on the mittens. Press in place with a hot, dry iron.

Step 4 With three strands of black embroidery floss or one strand of #8 Perle cotton buttonhole-stitch the shapes to the mittens, using a nice, even stitch. Refer to General Instructions for the Decorative Stitch diagrams.

I found wonderful old wool mittens knit with not-so-wonderful colors. To turn unattractively-colored mittens into the warm scarlet color, I used a water-based dye to achieve this dark, rich shade of red, following the manufacturer's instructions but using only five quarts of water. Lay the wool mittens out flat to dry thoroughly before adding appliqués and trims.

Mitten Snowman Body

Trace onto fusible web

Mitten Star

Trace onto fusible web

Mitten Tree

Trace onto fusible web

Step 5 With six strands of embroidery floss or two strands of #8 Perle cotton, stitch French knots for the snow. With three strands of floss or one strand of #8 Perle cotton, stitch French knots for eyes and nose on the snowman mittens. Make French knots for the ornaments on the tree mittens.

Step 6 Referring to the photograph, outline-stitch the snowmam's arms with gold embroidery floss or two strands of #8 Perle cotton.

Step 7 For the snowman's mouth, use the running stitch with three strands of embroidery floss or one strand of #8 Perle cotton.

YO-YO MUG MATS

Fabrics and Supplies
• 9, 4-inch squares of coordinating homespun plaids for yo-yos template material

Step 1 Trace a 3-inch diameter circle onto template material for the yo-yo and cut it out.

Step 2 Trace around the template on the wrong side of the fabric squares.

Step 3 Turn the edges of each circle under 1/8-inch, judging this distance by eye. Take care to keep the seam allowances of each circle the same size. Use one strand of quilting thread to make running stitches close to the fold. Make these stitches approximately 1/4-inch long and 1/4-inch apart.

Step 4 To form each yo-yo, pull up the gathering thread so that the circle is gathered on the right side. Take a few stitches through the gathered folds and knot the thread. Clip the threads close to the fabric. The back side of the yo-yo will be flat.

Step 5 Stitch the yo-yos together with fine whip stitches at the outer edges. To do so, place the yo-yos right sides together and whip-stitch about a 1/8-inch section. Make a secure knot and clip the thread. Continue adding yo-yos in this fashion.

Step 6 Stitch yo-yos together in rows.

Just like the pioneers, nothing goes to waste in our household. Leftover yo-yos make quick and easy mug mats— perfect stocking stuffers or last-minute gifts!

HE'S ALL HEART SANTA ORNAMENT

Fabrics and Supplies

- 1/4 yard RED PRINT for Santa's hat and body
- 1-1/2 x 7-inch piece BLACK PRINT for belt
- 4 x 8-inch piece muslin for head
- 1 package wool roving for beard and hair
- Black Pigma® fine tip permanent marker for facial features
- Blush for cheek color
- 1/2-inch jingle bell
- Fiberfill for stuffing
- #8 gold Perle cotton or embroidery floss
- 22-inch piece 19-gauge wire for greenery hanger
- 30-inch piece 1/2-inch-wide artificial wire garland for greenery hanger

Making the heart body

Step 1   From the RED PRINT fabric cut two heart shapes for body.

Step 2   From the BLACK PRINT fabric cut a 1-1/2 x 7-inch strip for belt.

Step 3   For the belt, fold both long edges of the black fabric to the center of the strip, wrong sides together, and press.

Step 4   Position the belt on the right side of one body piece as indicated on pattern. Stitch in place.

Step 5   Using two strands of #8 gold Perle cotton (or six strands of embroidery floss) stitch the "buckle" using simple long straight stitches. Refer to diagram on Santa's body pattern piece.

Step 6   With right sides together, stitch the body pieces together, leaving a 3-inch opening at the top for stuffing purposes.

Step 7   Stuff with fiberfill and hand-stitch opening closed.

Making the head and hat

Step 1   Cut two head shapes from the muslin fabric.

The design of my Santa ornament suggests that "he's all heart," expressing the sentiment of the season perfectly. Use it for an ornament for the tree or add a little "heart" to your gift-wrapping.

Step 2   With right sides together stitch the two pieces together, leaving the bottom edge open for stuffing purposes.

Step 3   Stuff with fiberfill and hand-stitch opening closed.

Step 4   Hand-stitch the head to the body. Mark eyes and nose with Pigma® marking pen. Use blush to make rosy cheeks.

Step 5   Hot-glue wool roving for beard and hair all around the head. Add enough wool roving to the head so the hat is filled out with wool "fluff." Fluff beard and hair so they are nice and full, and trimmed short enough so buckle and belt will show.

Step 6   From the red print fabric cut 2 hat shapes.

Step 7   With right sides together, stitch the two hat pieces together leaving the bottom open. Turn right side out. Turn raw edge under 1/2-inch, and press (no need to topstitch).

Step 8 Attach hat with hot glue or hand tack. If it appears too large, more wool should be put on the head to fill it out.

Step 9 Flop top of hat forward, pleat the end a bit and tack to the edge of the hat. Add a small jingle bell to the point of the hat.

Attaching greenery hanger

Insert the 19-gauge wire at seam just above the belt and through to the opposite seam, exiting at the same position above the belt. Form a nice circle above the Santa and twist the ends together. Wrap the artificial wire garland around the wire hanger.

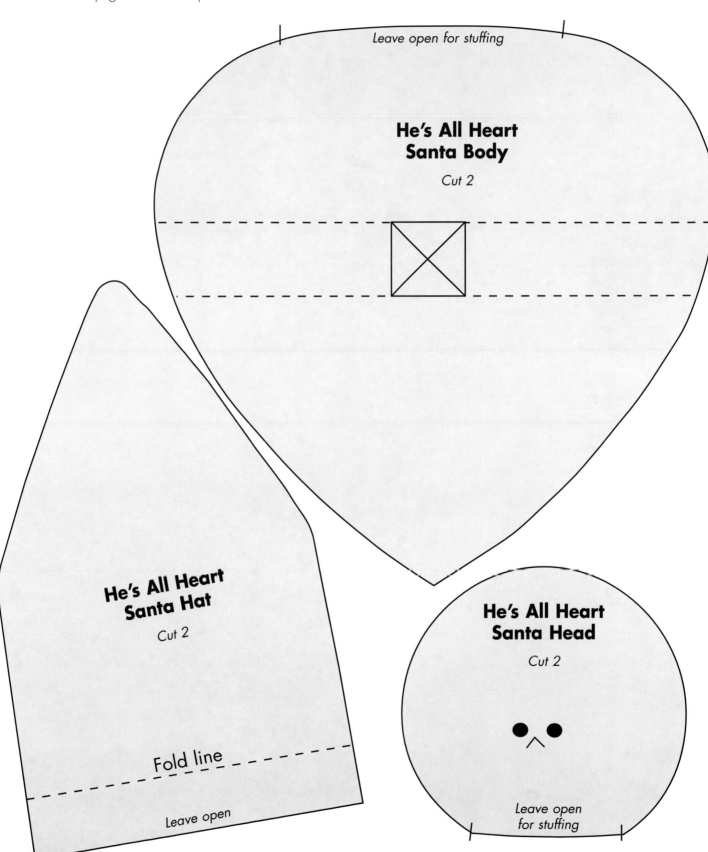

Leave open for stuffing

He's All Heart Santa Body

Cut 2

He's All Heart Santa Hat

Cut 2

Fold line

Leave open

He's All Heart Santa Head

Cut 2

Leave open for stuffing

ALL WRAPPED UP

Gift-giving has never been easier with new packaging options like rubber stamps and unpainted papier-maché boxes inspired by antiques like the church shown opposite. Lynette discovered this tiny 2-inch treasure in a box of ornaments purchased at an auction. For small gifts, use stacking star boxes decorated with holly and glitter. For instant wrapping paper, begin by working on a large piece of brown kraft paper. Practice stenciling the holly and berry motifs on the paper, dust with glitter, and allow them to dry without smudging. Paint the gift boxes for a galaxy of stars.

Christmas Eve

CELEBRATING HOLIDAY TRADITION

At our house, Christmas Eve is a special evening which includes coming home from the 11:00 p.m. service at church to share a late dessert in the living room. Weeks before, however, the living room has been transformed into a fairyland of lights and decorations. Soft accents like quilts and stockings are in traditional red and green, contrasting nicely with the black-and-cream upholstery.

CHECKERBOARD RUFFLED PILLOW

14-inches square

Fabrics and Supplies

Yardage is based on 42-inch wide fabric

- 1/8 yard RED PRINT for checkerboard
- 1/8 yard BEIGE PRINT checkerboard
- 7/8 yard GREEN PRINT for border and pillow back
- 1/3 yard RED/BLACK PRINT for ruffle
- 1/2 yard muslin for backing of pillow top
- Quilt batting, at least 16-inches square
- A rotary cutter, mat, and wide clear plastic ruler with 1/8-inch markings.

Festive holiday prints and deep green and berry red prints from the Thimbleberries® collection blend beautifully with black-and-cream fabrics for a classic country look that still says Christmas.

Pillow Top

Cutting

From RED PRINT:
- Cut 1, 2-1/2 x 42-inch strip.

From BEIGE PRINT:
- Cut 1, 2-1/2 x 42-inch strip.

From GREEN PRINT:
- Cut 2, 2-1/2 x 42-inch strips.
  From these strips cut:
  2, 2-1/2 x 10-1/2-inch border strips;
  2, 2-1/2 x 14-1/2-inch border strips.

Piecing

Step 1 Aligning long edges, sew the 2-1/2 x 42-inch RED and BEIGE strips together; press. Cut the strip set into segments.

Crosscut 15, 2-1/2-inch wide segments

Step 2 Sew 3, Step 1 segments together; press. Remove a 2-1/2-inch RED square from the end.

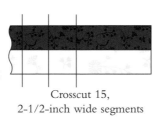
Make 3

Step 3 Sew 3, Step 1 segments together; press. Remove a 2-1/2-inch BEIGE square from the end.

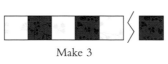
Make 2

Step 4 Sew together the Step 2 and Step 3 strips, and press. At this point the checkerboard block should measure 10-1/2-inches square.

Step 5 Sew a 2-1/2 x 10-1/2-inch GREEN border strip to the top and bottom of the checkerboard block, and press. Sew a 2-1/2 x 14-1/2-inch GREEN border strip to the sides of the checkerboard block, and press.

Putting It All Together

Step 1 Trim the muslin backing and batting so they are 2-inches larger than the pillow top dimensions.

Step 2 Layer the muslin backing, batting, and pillow top. Baste these layers together and quilt.

Step 3 When quilting is complete, trim the excess batting and backing even with the pillow top.

Note: To prepare the pillow top before attaching the ruffle, try hand basting the edges of all 3 layers of the pillow top together. This will prevent the edge of the pillow top from rippling when you attach the ruffle.

Pillow Ruffle

Cutting

From RED/BLACK PRINT:

• Cut 4, 5-1/2 x 42-inch ruffle strips.

Attaching the Ruffle

Step 1 Diagonally piece together the 5-1/2-inch wide RED/BLACK strips.

Step 2 With right sides facing, sew the short raw edges together with a diagonal seam to make a continuous ruffle strip. Trim the seam allowance to 1/4-inch, and press.

Step 3 Fold the strip in half lengthwise, wrong sides together, and press. Divide the ruffle strip into 4 equal segments, and mark the quarter points with safety pins.

Step 4 To gather the ruffle, position a heavy-weight thread (or 2 strands of regular weight sewing thread) 1/4-inch from the raw edge of the folded ruffle strip.

Note: You will need a length of thread 2 times the circumference of the pillow. Secure one end of the heavy thread by stitching across it. Then zigzag stitch over the thread all the way around the ruffle strip, taking care not to sew through the thread.

⌐ Fold ⌐

└ Raw edges ┘

Step 5 With right sides together, pin the ruffle to the pillow top, matching the quarter points of the ruffle to the corners of the pillow. Pin in place.

Step 6 Gently pull the gathering stitches until the ruffle fits the pillow top, taking care to allow a little extra ruffle at each corner for a full look. Pin in place, and machine-baste the ruffle to the pillow top, using a 1/4-inch seam allowance.

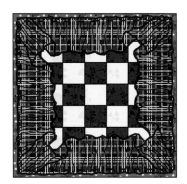

Pillow Back

Cutting

From GREEN PRINT:

• Cut 2, 14-1/2 x 18-1/2-inch rectangles.

Assembling the Pillow Back

Step 1 With wrong sides together, fold the 14-1/2 x 18-1/2-inch GREEN rectangles in half to form 2, 9 x 14-1/2-inch double-thick pillow back pieces.

Step 2 Overlap the 2 folded edges by about 4-inches so that the pillow back measures 14-1/2-inches square, and pin. Stitch around the entire pillow back to create a single pillow back.

Overlap

Fold

Step 3 With right sides together, layer the pillow back and the pillow top, and pin. The ruffle will be turned toward the center of the pillow at this time. Stitch around the outside edge, using a 3/8-inch seam allowance.

Step 4 Trim the pillow back and corner seam allowances if needed. Turn the pillow right side out and fluff up the ruffle. Insert the pillow form through the back opening.

BACK HOME COVERLET

81 x 95-inches

Fabrics and Supplies

Yardage is based on 42-inch wide fabric

- 1-3/4 yards GOLD PRINT for centers, triangles, and lattice posts
- 1-5/8 yards BLACK PRINT for log cabin strips and inner border
- 4-1/4 yards GREEN PRINT for log cabin strips, lattice, and outer border
- 2-1/4 yards RED PRINT for log cabin strips
- 7/8 yard GOLD PRINT for binding
- 5-5/8 yards backing fabric
- Quilt batting, at least 85 x 99-inches
- A rotary cutter, mat, and wide clear plastic ruler with 1/8-inch markings.

Log Cabin Block (Make 30)

Cutting

From GOLD PRINT:

- Cut 3, 3-1/2 x 42-inch strips.
  From these strips cut:
  30, 3-1/2-inch squares.
- Cut 18, 2 x 42-inch strips.
  From these strips cut:
  360, 2-inch squares.

From BLACK PRINT:

- Cut 6, 2 x 42-inch strips.
  From these strips cut:
  60, 2 x 3-1/2-inch rectangles.
- Cut 10, 2 x 42-inch strips. From these strips cut:
  60, 2 x 6-1/2-inch rectangles.

From GREEN PRINT:

- Cut 10, 2 x 42-inch strips. From these strips cut:
  60, 2 x 6-1/2-inch rectangles.
- Cut 15, 2 x 42-inch strips. From these strips cut:
  60, 2 x 9-1/2-inch rectangles.

From RED PRINT:

- Cut 15, 2 x 42-inch strips. From these strips cut:
  60, 2 x 9-1/2-inch rectangles.
- Cut 20, 2 x 42-inch strips. From these strips cut:
  60, 2 x 12-1/2-inch rectangles.

For the holidays, I enhance the country colors already in the living room with soft accents like the "Back Home" coverlet. The log cabin motif features coordinating fabrics in red, black, and green with corner blocks in deep golds. Muted black prints and a gold binding tie it all together to coordinate the quilt with existing furnishings.

Assembling the Log Cabin Blocks

Step 1   Sew a 2 x 3-1/2-inch BLACK rectangle to both sides of a 3-1/2-inch GOLD square. Press seam allowances toward the BLACK fabric.

Make 30

Step 2   Position a 2-inch GOLD square on the corners of a 2 x 6-1/2-inch BLACK rectangle. Draw a diagonal line from corner to corner on the GOLD squares. Stitch on the lines. Trim away corners leaving a scant 1/4-inch seam allowance. Press seam allowances toward the BLACK fabric.

Make 60

Step 3 Sew a unit from Step 2 to the top and bottom of the Step 1 unit. Press seam allowances toward the BLACK fabric. At this point the block should measure 6-1/2-inches square.

Make 30

Step 4 Sew a 2 x 6-1/2-inch GREEN rectangle to both sides of the block. Press seam allowances toward the GREEN fabric.

Step 5 Position a 2-inch GOLD square on the corners of a 2 x 9-1/2-inch GREEN rectangle. Draw a diagonal line from corner to corner on the GOLD squares. Stitch on the lines. Trim away corners leaving a scant 1/4-inch seam allowance. Press seam allowances toward the GREEN fabric.

Make 60

Step 6 Sew a unit from Step 5 to the top and bottom of the block. Press seam allowances toward the GREEN fabric. At this point the block should measure 9-1/2-inches square.

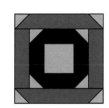

Step 7 Sew a 2 x 9-1/2-inch RED rectangle to both sides of the block. Press seam allowances toward the RED fabric.

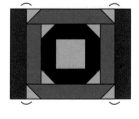

Step 8 Position a 2-inch GOLD square on the corners of a 2 x 12-1/2-inch RED rectangle. Draw a diagonal line from corner to corner on the GOLD squares. Stitch on the line. Trim away corners leaving a scant 1/4-inch seam allowance. Press seam allowances toward the RED fabric.

Make 60

Step 9 Sew a unit from Step 8 to the top and bottom of the block. Press seam allowances toward the RED fabric. At this point the block should measure 12-1/2-inches square.

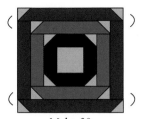

Make 30
Log Cabin Blocks

Quilt Center

Cutting

From GREEN PRINT:
- Cut 24, 2 x 42-inch strips. From these strips cut: 71, 2 x 12-1/2-inch lattice strips.

From GOLD PRINT:
- Cut 3, 2 x 42-inch strips. From these strips cut: 42, 2-inch squares for lattice posts.

Assembling the Quilt Center

Step 1 Assemble the lattice strips. Each strip is made up of 5, 2 x 12-1/2-inch GREEN strips and 6, 2-inch GOLD lattice posts. Sew the strips and lattice posts together. Press seam allowances toward the GREEN fabric.

Make 7

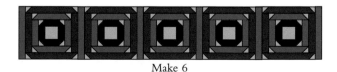

Step 2 Sew 5 log cabin blocks and 6 GREEN lattice strips together to form each block row. Press seam allowances toward the GREEN fabric. At this point each row should measure 69-1/2-inches long.

Make 6

Step 3 Pin the block rows to the lattice strips. Sew the block rows and lattice strips together to make the quilt center. Press seam allowances toward the lattice strips. At this point the quilt center should measure 69-1/2- x 83-inches.

Borders

Note: The yardage given allows for the border strips to be cut on the crosswise grain. Diagonally piece the strips as needed.

Cutting

From BLACK PRINT:
- Cut 8, 2 x 42-inch strips for inner border.

From GREEN PRINT:
- Cut 9, 5 x 42-inch strips for outer border.

Attaching the Borders

Step 1 For the inner border, measure the quilt from left to right, through the middle, to determine the length of the top and bottom borders. Cut 2, 2-inch wide BLACK strips to this length. Sew the borders to the quilt, and press.

Step 2 Measure the quilt from top to bottom, through the middle, to determine the length of the side borders. Cut 2, 2-inch wide BLACK strips to this length. Sew the borders to the quilt, and press.

Step 3 For the outer border, measure the quilt as in Step 1. Cut 2, 5-inch wide GREEN strips to this length. Sew the borders to the top and bottom of the quilt, and press.

Step 4 Measure the quilt as in Step 2. Cut 2, 5-inch wide GREEN strips to this length. Sew the borders to the sides of the quilt, and press.

Putting It All Together

Step 1 Cut the 5-5/8 yard length of backing in half crosswise to make 2, 2-3/4 yard lengths. Trim the backing and batting so they are 4-inches larger than the quilt top.

Step 2 Mark the quilt top for quilting. Layer the backing, batting, and quilt top. Baste the 3 layers together and quilt.

Step 3 When quilting is complete, hand-baste the 3 layers together a scant 1/4-inch from the edge. This hand basting keeps the layers from shifting and prevents puckers from forming when adding the binding. Trim excess batting and backing even with the edge of the quilt top.

Binding

Cutting

From GOLD PRINT:
- Cut 9, 2-3/4 x 42-inch strips.

Step 1 Diagonally piece the strips together. Fold the strip in half lengthwise, wrong sides together, and press.

Step 2 With raw edges of the binding and quilt top even, stitch with a 3/8-inch seam allowance.

Step 3 Miter binding at the corners. To do so, stop sewing 3/8-inch from the corner of the quilt. Flip the binding strip up and away from the quilt, then fold the binding down even with the raw edge of the quilt. Begin sewing at the upper edge. Miter all 4 corners in this manner.

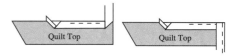

Step 4 Bring the folded edge of the binding to the back of the quilt and hand sew the binding in place.

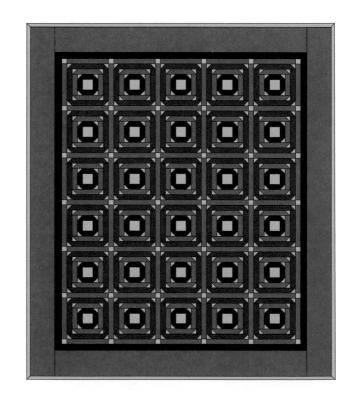

WINTERTIME WHITES

Long ago, Lynette gave herself permission to mix several styles of cupboards and wardrobes in various types of woods for her own brand of classic country decorating. At Christmastime she opens the doors of the wardrobes and cupboards to display her collections of coordinating keepsakes and quilts.

The antique quilt shown above is "Seven Sisters" from the early 1900's. Lynette chooses her favorite Santas and combines them with antique white pitchers, vases, and fresh greens. She tops it all off with antique winter white mica covered churches.

The antique jelly cupboard, now filled with quilts, is adorned with a smaller cupboard filled with stoneware milk/cream pitchers, each of which has a different handle detail. The glass cream pitchers on the cupboard have a detail reminiscent of a tree. Lynette fills each with a fragrant votive to give a warm candle glow to the pitcher arrangement.

RAG WREATH

10-inch diameter

Fabrics and supplies

Yardage based on 45-inch wide fabric

- 1-1/2 yards homespun plaid fabric
- 1 foam wreath, 10-inch diameter
- #8 red Perle cotton or embroidery floss
- #8 black Perle cotton or embroidery floss
- 12-inch square black wool for appliqué background
- 6-inch square green wool for leaves
- 6-inch square gold wool for stars
- 3-inch square red wool for hearts

Wreath

Step 1   Tear twelve 2-1/2-inch wide homespum plaid strips crossgrain. Pull off loose threads to get the ragged, fringe look.

Step 2   Seam these torn strips together end to end to make one long continuous strip. Wrap into a rag ball for ease in handling when wrapping around foam wreath. Strips are slightly scrunched and not kept perfectly flat.

Step 3   Wrap foam wreath with the homespun plaid strips, overlapping the strips. Make sure wreath is well covered. Continue wrapping until all fabric is used. Secure with a straight pin.

Step 4   Tear eight 2-1/2-inch wide homespun plaid strips crossgrain. Cut these strips into 13-inch long pieces. Fringe the edges and sides a little. Wrap each homespun plaid strip around the wreath and tie into a knot, spacing knots 3/4-inch apart.

A small rag wreath does double-duty in the living room. Repeating the black-and-cream theme of the upholstery, it also proves that you don't always have to hang a wreath on a wall. While only 10-inches in diameter, this wreath is small but mighty when attached to the side of a Christmas-red basket.

Stars and Holly Leaves

Step 1   From templates given, cut 4 green leaves, 3 gold stars, and 3 red hearts.

Step 2   Layer the red hearts on the centers of the gold stars. With black Perle cotton, buttonhole-stitch the heart edges to the stars. Refer to General Instructions for the Decorative Stitch diagrams.

Step 3 Layer the gold star onto a 3-inch black wool square. With black Perle cotton, buttonhole-stitch the edges to the black wool. When you have finished stitching, trim excess black wool away leaving a 1/4-inch black wool edging around star. Place this unit on black wool and cut out a second piece of black wool for backing of star. Using red Perle cotton, buttonhole-stitch the raw edges together.

Step 4 Layer the green leaves on a 3 x 4-inch piece of black wool. With black Perle cotton, buttonhole-stitch the edges to the black wool using a nice, even stitch. When you have finished stitching, trim excess black wool away leaving a 1/4-inch black wool edging around leaf. Place this unit on black wool and cut out a second piece of black wool for backing of leaf. Using red Perle cotton, buttonhole-stitch the raw edges together.

Step 5 Glue or stitch leaves and star on wreath as shown.

Step 6 Attach a thread loop through fabric on back of wreath for hanging.

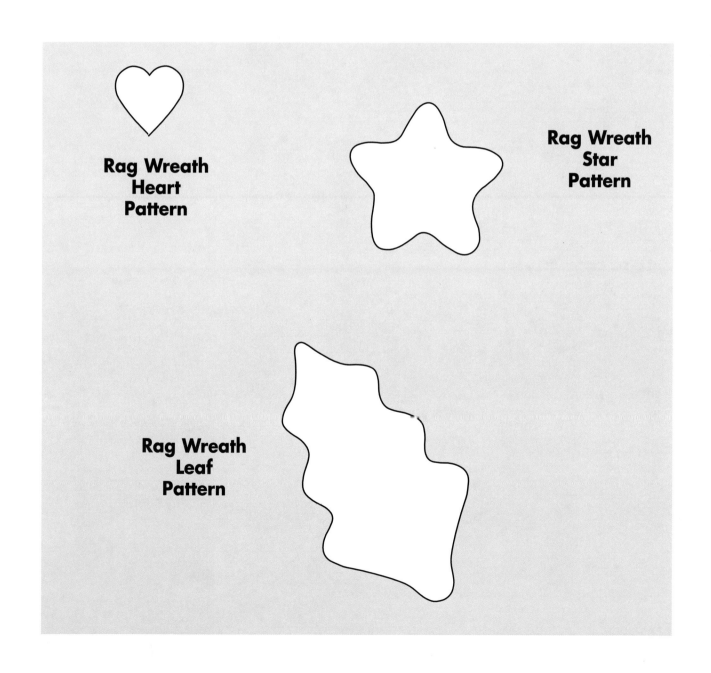

Rag Wreath Heart Pattern

Rag Wreath Star Pattern

Rag Wreath Leaf Pattern

COUNTRY CUPBOARDS

Adding greens and holly turns everyday cupboards into instant holiday attractions. The matching recessed cabinets original to the house flank a low table also trimmed for the holidays with a basket of greens and a star-topped lattice tree fashioned from cast iron after traditional wooden Scandinavian lattice trees. In Colonial times, fruit symbolized bounty and festivity and was a rare commodity in the wintertime. To celebrate, adults garlanded their houses with strings of cranberries and dried apples, while children delighted in the traditional orange or apple found in the toe of their stockings on Christmas morning.

To tie the cupboards together visually, Lynette chose a unifying theme—in this case, vintage 1940's Blue Ridge Crab Apple dishes, vases, and flower-pots interspersed with miniature ladder-back and Windsor chairs.

70

ORNAMENTS

An unusually large feather tree easily accommodates Lynette's growing collection of glass ball ornaments. Most of the collection shown here came from her mother. Lynette continues to add to the collection when she finds ornaments that are the same vintage. And, as with most collectibles, finding them in the original boxes adds to their value.

The Santa shown below is actually an antique ornament from the early 1900's that is quite fragile. When it proved to be too large for her tree, Lynette decided to frame it for display. The ornament floats on a mat and spacers are used before the two outer mats are added which allows room for the dimensional quality of the Santa.

The glittering framed Santa rests on a tabletop and is surrounded by antique tinsel and glass pine cone ornaments in pastel colors to coordinate with the silver tinsel surrounding the Santa ornament.

MIDNIGHT CELEBRATION

After the 11:00 p.m. service at their church, Lynette and Neil gather with close family members in the living room for dessert. When dessert is served, Lynette sets the table with fresh flowers to match the white accents in the room, silver service that once belonged to Neil's great-grandmother, and a handcrafted and painted candlestick holder adapted by a friend from a Swedish antique.

More candlesticks filled with white candles grace the mantel trimmed with greens filled with dried hydrangea and berry sprigs. The antique star and bells are covered with red chenille roping. When Lynette found the bells in an attic they were black— covered with layers of dust which she carefully removed to reveal the red chenille roping.

Dessert is served in green Depression glass dishes from Neil's mother. For recipes, please turn the page.

BROWN SUGAR SHORTBREAD

1 cup butter

1/2 cup brown sugar

pinch of salt

1 teaspoon vanilla

1 1/2 cups flour

1/2 cup chopped pecans
(optional)

Cream sugar, butter and vanilla.
Add salt and flour. Mix to make
a firm dough. Press into a well-
buttered 9-inch square pan or
pie plate. Pierce with fork
for traditional shortbread
appearance. Bake at 350° for
20 minutes. Makes 16 squares
or 8 slices.

HOT FUDGE SAUCE

6 ounces semi-sweet chocolate chips

1/2 cup butter

1 large can evaporated milk

3-1/2 cups powdered sugar

1 teaspoon of vanilla

Bring mixture to a simmer on medium heat
and stir while cooking for 8–10 minutes.
Mix with wire whisk until smooth. Add vanilla.
Serve warm over peppermint stick ice cream.
Makes 1 pint.

Christmas Day

GOOD CHEER, FOOD, AND FRIENDS

On Christmas morning I serve a hearty breakfast. Later, since our house overlooks the Crow River we gather up skates, mittens, and scarves, and take along fingerfood snacks and hot cider. A toboggan serves as a tabletop for a pleasant afternoon of skating. Neil and I are often joined by our grown son and daughter— Matt (standing beside us), his friend, Cinammon (seated), and newlyweds, Kerry and Trevor (standing).

OATMEAL MUFFINS

1/2 cup oil

1/2 cup brown sugar, packed

1 egg

1 cup buttermilk

1 cup quick oats

1 cup flour

1 teaspoon baking powder

1/2 teaspoon salt

1/2 teaspoon baking soda

Mix all ingredients and spoon batter into greased muffin tins 2/3 full. Bake at 400° for 15–20 minutes. Remove from oven and dust with powdered sugar. Cool 10 minutes and remove muffins from tin.
Makes 12 muffins.

GRANOLA

6 cups old-fashioned oats

1 cup sunflower seeds

1/2 cup sesame seeds

1 cup coconut

1 tablespoon cinnamon

1/2 cup walnuts

1/2 cup chopped pecans

Mix the above ingredients together in 9 x 13-inch pan.

1/4 cup oil

1/2 cup honey

1 teaspoon vanilla

Mix together oil and honey in saucepan or microwave until the mixture just boils. Add 1 teaspoon vanilla.

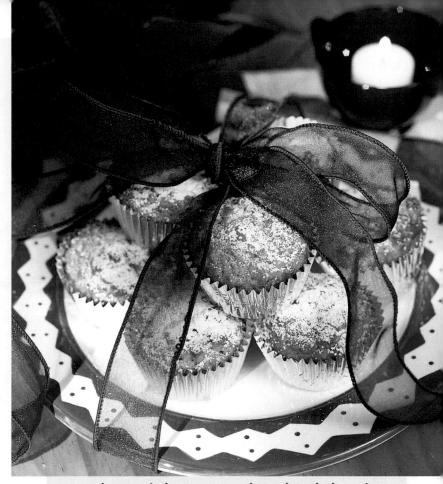

The spirit of Christmas comes alive in the early dawn of Christmas morning when the breakfast table is aglow with candles and red, white, and green table accents. Vintage linens, glasses, bowls, and jars are mixed with new Christmas plates. Hearty fare includes oatmeal muffins and homemade granola topped with craisins served in a spooner— a footed goblet-like glass that traditionally held spoons on kitchen tables, a practice quite common long ago. The smaller spooner is a cherished piece that was always on my Grandmother's kitchen table.

Pour the honey mixture over the oat mixture. Stir until the oat mixture is well coated. Bake at 325° for 10 minutes. Take the pan out of the oven and stir the mixture well so browning will be uniform. Put the pan back in the oven and continue this process until you achieve the desired browning. Total browning time is approximately 1/2 hour. Serve with raisins or craisins which should be added after baking. Top with a sprinkling of raw sugar.

GIFT BAG
7 x 14-1/2-inches

Fabrics and Supplies
Yardage is based on 42-inch-wide fabric

- 1/2 yard RED PRINT for gift bag

- 3/8 yard RED PLAID for trim (cut on bias)

- A rotary cutter, mat, and wide clear plastic ruler with 1/8-inch markings

Cutting
From RED PRINT:

- Cut 1,15-inch square.

From RED PLAID:

- Cut enough 6-inch wide bias strips to make a 15-inch long strip.

Piecing

Step 1 Diagonally piece the 6-inch wide RED PLAID bias strips as needed. Fold the strip in half lengthwise, wrong sides together, and press.

Step 2 With right sides together and raw edges even, stitch the 3-inch wide RED PLAID trim strip to the 15-inch RED PRINT square with a 1-inch seam allowance.

Step 3 Turn the folded edge of the trim over the raw edges and to the wrong side of the RED PRINT fabric so that the stitching line does not show. Topstitch in place.

Guests often ask for the granola recipe, and I send it home with them, along with a sampler supply in a gift bag stitched up from vintage tablecloths also used to make the napkins.

Step 4 With right sides together, fold the trimmed rectangle in half and sew the raw edges together using a 1/4-inch seam allowance. Turn the bag right side out.

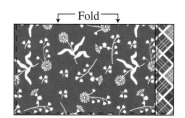

Fold

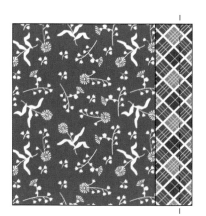

HOT SPICY CIDER

Combine:

1/2 cup brown sugar

1/4 teaspoon salt

2 quarts cider

Combine spices in spice ball:

1 teaspoon whole allspice

1 teaspoon whole cloves

3-inch cinnamon stick

dash of nutmeg

Add to cider, and slowly bring to boil.
Cover and simmer 20 minutes. Serve hot.
Makes 10 servings.

*For skating parties and other outdoor festivities, I like to bring
along plenty of hot spicy cider and quick-energy snacks like
chocolate chip bars. Cutting the bars into bite-size squares and
inserting a party pick into each one makes it easy for skaters
to glide by and grab a snack without even removing a mitten!*

CHOCOLATE CHIP BARS

1/4 cup butter, room temperature

1 cup light brown sugar

1 egg

3/4 cup flour

1 teaspoon baking powder

1/2 teaspoon salt

1/2 teaspoon vanilla

1/2 cup nuts, chopped

1/2 cup chocolate chips

Cream butter and brown sugar until light and fluffy. Add
egg, vanilla and mix. Add flour, baking powder and salt;
mix thoroughly. Add chocolate chips and nuts. Bake in a
well-greased 8-inch square pan at 350° for 20 minutes.
Cut into 16, 2-inch squares.

WINTERTIME FUN

Lynette finds that a bench in the back entry is a great place for keeping winter gear handy—especially a supply of mittens.

Many of the hand-knitted mittens Lynette packs into the box are decorating accents when trimmed with treasures from her vintage button collection. She keeps them neat and tidy in an old wooden box painted red and stenciled with mittens, snowflakes, and stars.

The wintertime stencil motifs are repeated on floor cloth canvas which can be generously-sized to use as a floor cloth to match the wooden mitten box or scaled down to use as a centerpiece/table runner on the kitchen table.

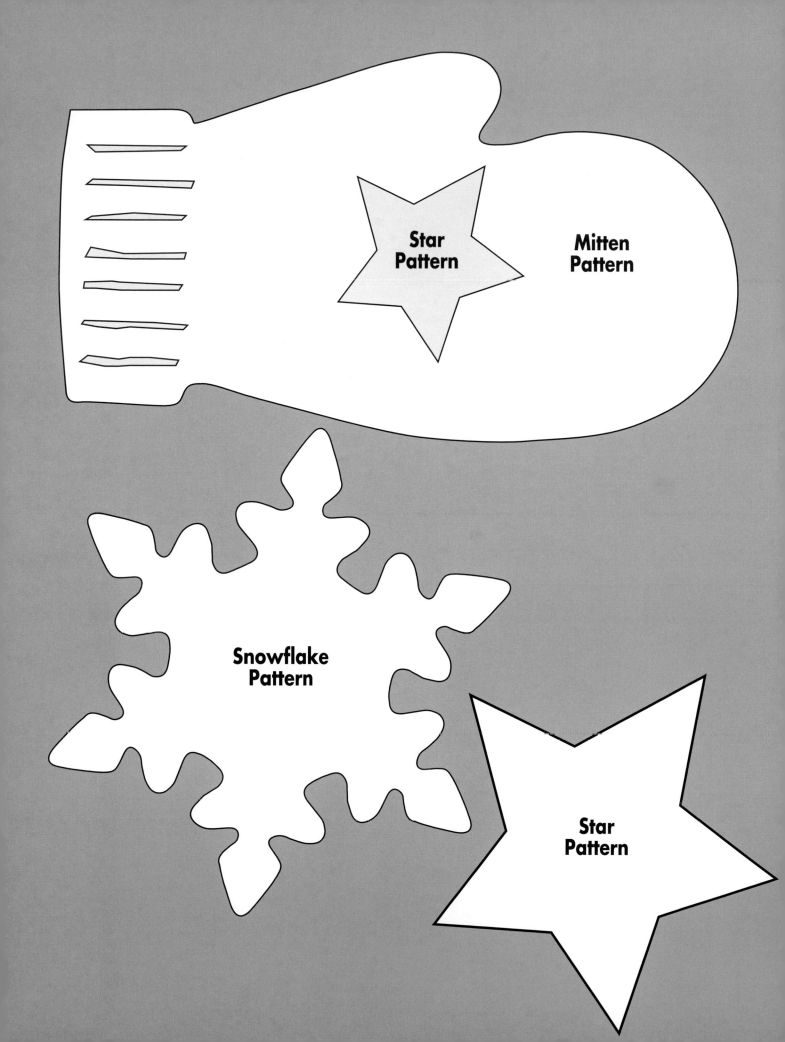

Star Pattern

Mitten Pattern

Snowflake Pattern

Star Pattern

SWEDISH NUTS

1-1/2 pounds pecan halves

2 egg whites

1 cup sugar

1/2 cup butter

Toast pecans in a 350° oven for 15 minutes.

Beat egg whites until stiff and add 1 cup sugar slowly to dissolve sugar as you are beating. Fold meringue and nuts together making sure all are evenly coated. Melt 1/2 cup butter in jelly roll pan and mix meringué covered nuts with butter. Bake at 350° for 30 minutes. Salt to taste. Cool and store in an air tight container. Use as candied nuts for a snack or as garnish in a salad.

Fresh air and outdoor wintertime fun require good food and lots of it. My family loves to come in from an afternoon of skating to a salad and casserole meal that I can prepare ahead of time. That way, I can join in the fun, too! Make-ahead ingredients include the Swedish nuts for the red pear and Romaine salad, and the artichoke chicken pasta which bakes up quickly in a 400-degree oven in a mere 30 minutes.

CROSTINI

1 large loaf French bread

1/2 cup olive oil

1/2 cup butter

Slice bread into 1-inch diagonal slices. Melt olive oil and butter. With a pastry brush coat one side of each slice. Place bread on a cookie sheet and bake at 300° for 1/2 hour until toasted.

ARTICHOKE CHICKEN PASTA

3 cups cooked diced turkey or chicken

1 can artichokes in water, drained, cut up

1 teaspoon minced dried onions

1/4 teaspoon Tabasco®

1/4 teaspoon marjoram

1 (10 1/4 oz.) can cream of chicken soup

1/2 cup mayonnaise

1/2 cup sour cream

1 (13 oz.) can evaporated milk

1 cup mozzarella cheese, grated

1 clove garlic, crushed

1 (12 oz.) package bow tie pasta, prepared according to package directions and rinsed under cold water

1 cup grated cheddar cheese

1 cup grated parmesan cheese

Mix all ingredients reserving 1/2 cup parmesan cheese and 1 cup cheddar cheese. Place in a greased 9 x 13-inch baking dish. Sprinkle parmesan and cheddar cheese over top. Bake 30 minutes at 400° or until hot and bubbly. Garnish with paprika and parsley. Makes 8–10 servings.

GOOD CHEER

Lynette's kitchen is a welcoming place year-round with a bright and cheery decorating theme of blue, cream, and yellow.

For Christmas she magically transforms cupboards and counter-tops by substituting red pottery for the yellow and adding a sprinkling of greens, holly, berries, and pine cones.

On the center island, Lynette creates a quick but impressive centerpiece by stacking a bowl on an inverted larger bowl to raise the candle. Before adding the smaller bowl, she places a wreath on the inverted bowl. Resting inside the wreath, the smaller bowl holds a glass chimney filled with miniature apples and a candle. Both are then trimmed with a unifiying garland of miniature apples.

CHURN DASH QUILT

60-1/2-inches square

Fabrics and Supplies

Yardage is based on 42-inch-wide fabric

- 1/4 yard each of 25 assorted BLUE PRINTS for blocks
- 1/4 yard each of 25 assorted CREAM PRINTS for blocks
- 1-2/3 yards DARK BLUE PRINT for lattice and border
- 5/8 yard DARK BLUE PRINT for binding
- 3-3/4 yards backing fabric
- Quilt batting, at least 65-inches square
- A rotary cutter, mat, and wide clear plastic ruler with 1/8-inch markings

Churn Dash Blocks (Make 25)

Cutting

From each Assorted BLUE PRINT:

- Cut 1, 3-7/8 x 10-inch strip.
- Cut 1, 2 x 16-inch strip.

From each Assorted CREAM PRINT:

- Cut 1, 3-7/8 x 10-inch strip.
- Cut 1, 3-1/2-inch square.
- Cut 1, 2 x 16-inch strip.

Piecing

The instructions that follow are for one Block.

Step 1   Layer a 3-7/8 x 10-inch BLUE strip with a 3-7/8 x 10-inch CREAM strip. Press together, but do not sew. Cut the layered strip into squares.

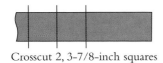

Crosscut 2, 3-7/8-inch squares

Step 2   Cut the layered squares in half diagonally. Stitch 1/4-inch from the diagonal edge of each pair of triangles, and press. At this point each triangle-pieced square should measure 3-1/2-inches square.

Make 4, 3-1/2-inch triangle-pieced squares

Step 3   Aligning long edges, sew a 2 x 16-inch BLUE and CREAM strip together, and press. Cut the strip set into segments.

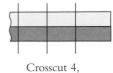

Crosscut 4,
3-1/2-inch wide segments

Step 4   Sew a Step 2 triangle-pieced square to both sides of a Step 3 segment, and press.

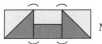
Make 2

Step 5   Sew a Step 3 segment to both sides of a 3-1/2-inch CREAM square, and press.

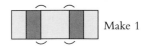
Make 1

Step 6   Sew a Step 4 segment to the top and bottom of a Step 5 segment, and press. At
this point the block should measure
9-1/2-inches square.

Make 1

Step 7   Repeat Step 1 through 6 to make a total
of 25 Churn Dash blocks using the
assorted BLUE and CREAM PRINTS.

Quilt Center and Border

Note: Diagonally piece the strips together
as needed.

Cutting

From DARK BLUE PRINT:

- Cut 5, 3 x 42-inch strips. From these strips cut:
20, 3 x 9-1/2-inch lattice strips.
- Cut 12 more 3 x 42-inch strips for the long
lattice strips and border strips.

Assembling the Quilt Center and Attaching the Border

Step 1   Sew together 5 Churn Dash blocks and
4, 3 x 9-1/2-inch DARK BLUE lattice
strips, and press. Make 5 block rows. At
this point each block row should measure
9-1/2 x 55-1/2-inches.

Step 2   Cut 6, 3 x 55-1/2-inch DARK BLUE
lattice/top and bottom border strips.

Step 3   Sew together the 5 block rows and
4, 3 x 55-1/2-inch DARK BLUE lattice
strips to make the quilt center, and press.

Step 4   Sew the 2 remaining 3 x 55-1/2-inch
DARK BLUE top and bottom border strips
to the quilt, and press.

Step 5   Measure the quilt top from top to bottom,
through the middle, to determine the length
of the side borders. Cut 2, 3-inch wide
DARK BLUE strips to this length. Sew the
borders to the sides of the quilt, and press.

Putting It All Together

Step 1   Cut the 3-3/4 yard length of backing
fabric in half crosswise to form

2, 1-7/8 yard lengths. Remove the
selvages and sew the 2 lengths together,
and press. Trim the backing and batting so
they are 4-inches larger than the quilt top.

Step 2   Mark the quilt top for quilting. Layer the
backing, batting, and quilt top. Baste the
3 layers together and quilt.

Step 3   When the quilting is complete, hand-baste
the 3 layers together a scant 1/4-inch
from the raw edge. This hand basting
keeps the layers from shifting and prevents
puckers from forming when adding the
binding. Trim excess batting and backing
even with the edge of the quilt top.

Binding

Cutting

From DARK BLUE PRINT:

- Cut 7, 2-3/4 x 42-inch strips.

Step 1   Diagonally piece the strips together. Fold
the strip in half lengthwise, wrong sides
together, and press.

Step 2   With raw edges of the binding and quilt
top even, stitch with a 3/8-inch seam
allowance.

Step 3   Miter binding at the corners. To do so,
stop sewing 3/8-inch from the corner of
the quilt. Flip the binding strip up and
away from the quilt, then fold the binding
down even with the raw edge of the quilt.
Begin sewing at the upper edge. Miter all
4 corners in this manner.

Step 4   Bring the folded edge of the binding to the
back of the quilt and hand sew the
binding in place.

Candlelight
MAKING SPIRITS BRIGHT

*Formal dining calls for upscale country decorating, so for the dining room I chose
a soft antique red accented with lots of white, gold, and candlelight. White freshens a
holiday setting and provides a neutral background for reflecting candlelight off the
decorative accents placed around the room. All together, it makes for an enchanted place
for entertaining family and friends for a memorable evening not soon-to-be forgotten.*

WHITE CHRISTMAS

Keeping a softer decorating theme in mind, Lynette simply modifies the traditional red, green, and white of Christmas to a gentle cranberry, white, and a lighter shade of green and cream.

She begins by covering the dining table with an antique Damask tablecloth and napkins featuring holly, candles, and poinsettia motifs woven into the soft cranberry fabric. Mismatched antique dishes are a combination of green and white. The salad plates are tied with gold ribbon trimmed with pine cone ornaments as favors for the guests. For the center of the table, Lynette fills short antique green tumblers with votives. She then creates numerous small centerpiece arrangements of greens, holly, white lilies and mums in pink Depression glass vases and bowls. This keeps the tones similar between glassware and the tablecloth and napkins.

A wreath fills each of the windows sparkling against the night sky illuminated by hundreds of lights twinkling in the branches of the tree outside. On the bench below the windows, a white box built from ceiling panels overflows with greenery and pink wax flowers.

SIMPLE ACCENTS

For greater impact, Lynette creates a dozen of the same-style wreaths to fill the windows from the dining room through the kitchen and on into the family room for a unifying effect.

To save time, she begins with an artificial wreath and brightens it with easy-to-find materials. From late summer to early autumn Lynette gathers dried naturals including pine cones, yarrow, statice, and rose hips right in her own backyard. To assemble the wreath, she then wraps small bundles as shown below with florist tape, tops each with a pine cone and arranges the clusters as shown in the photograph above.

BRIGHT WHITES

Color comes softly to the corner of the dining room against a backdrop of off-white walls and a cream built-in corner cupboard.

To complete the soft decorating theme used throughout the room, Lynette fills the cupboard with cranberry, green, and white dishes from her collection and tucks a few greens in here and there. In the foreground, she fills an antique tabletop feather tree with glass pine cone ornaments in lighter shades of cranberry, blue, and gold.

In the opposite corner of the room, pine shelves hold white teapots embellished with cranberry flowers. On the small table, more white stoneware featuring clover, accents a large white pitcher. Lynette fills it with six inches of sand to secure the white candle and greens to match those in the planter box made from white tin ceiling panels, shown on page 94.

HOLIDAY BRIGHTS

Above the sideboard in the dining room, a handsome milkweed pod and magnolia leaf wreath brightened by dried white roses completes the green and white theme. As Lynette tops off the roses from her garden, she places them in a dish to dry. Interesting leaves can be left to dry in the same manner. She first wires the roses and then attaches them to the leaves using green florist tape.

In the glow of candlelight the pitcher and creamer become golden accents for the antique Christmas postcard framed in an old-fashioned swivel frame. Reproductions, like the antique one shown above, are readily available in gift stores.

Goodnight
SWEET DREAMS TO ALL

Since the holiday season can often be hectic, it's important to have a quiet retreat to rest, reflect, and refresh. In the upstairs of our home the bedrooms are decorated for Christmas with rest and relaxation in mind. Each of the bedrooms has its own special tree and a bed piled high with comforting quilts and pillows in classic country colors.

RUSTIC TRADITION

In the master bedroom, Lynette combines restful shades of deep red and forest green and brightens them with white accents throughout the room. The previous pages show a tree filled with Lynette's growing collection of handmade ornaments blended with white painted papier-maché stars, coated with diamond dust as well as several of the bouquets of fresh white flowers scattered about the room.

On the bed shown above, the standard decorating practice of combining prints, plaids and solids is updated with the addition of a charming vintage piece of Bark cloth depicting a snow scene used as a pillow front, with a wide band of printed fabric serving both as a border and a binding.

In the master bath, left, Lynette finds new life for an antique doll cradle now used for keeping towels right at hand, and an old green flower pot pressed into service as a candleholder.

FIRESIDE MEDALLION QUILT

Size: 38-inches square

Fabrics and Supplies

Yardage is based on 42-inch wide fabric

- 1/4 yard GOLD PRINT for center square and corner squares
- 3/4 yard BLACK PRINT for 9-patch block, block border, and outer border
- 1/4 yard RED PRINT for 9-patch block, inner border, and circle appliqués
- 5/8 yard GREEN PRINT for block border and swag appliqués
- 1 yard BLACK/BEIGE PLAID for middle border
- 1/2 yard RED PRINT for binding
- 1 yard paper-backed fusible web
- 1 skein black embroidery floss
- 1-1/4-inch yards backing fabric
- Quilt batting, at least 42-inch square
- A rotary cutter, mat, and wide clear plastic ruler with 1/8-inch markings

Cutting

From GOLD PRINT:
- Cut 1, 2-1/2-inch square for 9-patch block.
- Cut 4, 5-1/2-inch squares for corner squares.

From BLACK PRINT:
- Cut 8, 2-1/2-inch squares for 9-patch block and block border.
- Cut 4, 5-1/2 x 42-inch strips for outer border.

From RED PRINT:
- Cut 4, 2-1/2-inch squares for 9-patch block.
- Cut 1, 1-1/2 x 42-inch strip for inner border.

From GREEN PRINT:
- Cut 4, 2-1/2 x 6-1/2-inch rectangles for block borders.

From BLACK/BEIGE PLAID:
- Cut 4, 8 x 42-inch strips for middle border.

Piecing the 9-Patch Block

Step 1 Sew a 2-1/2-inch RED square to both sides of a 2-1/2-inch BLACK square, and press.

Make 2

Step 2 Sew a 2-1/2-inch BLACK square to both sides of a 2-1/2-inch GOLD square, and press.

Make 1

Step 3 Sew a Step 1 unit to both sides of a Step 2 unit to form the 9-patch block, and press.

Make 1

Step 4 Sew a 2-1/2 x 6-1/2-inch GREEN block border rectangle to the top and bottom of the 9-patch block, and press.

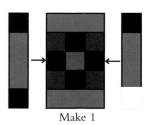
Make 1

103

Step 5 Add a 2-1/2-inch BLACK square to both ends of the remaining 2-1/2 x 6-1/2-inch GREEN rectangles. Sew the block borders to the sides of the 9-patch block, and press.

Attaching the Borders

Step 1 For the inner border measure the quilt from left to right, through the middle, to determine the length of the top and bottom borders. Cut 2, 1-1/2-inch wide RED strips to this length. Sew the borders to the top and bottom of the quilt, and press.

Step 2 Measure the quilt from top to bottom, through the center, to determine the length of the side borders. Cut 2, 1-1/2-inch wide RED strips to this length. Sew the borders to the sides of the quilt, and press.

Step 3 For the middle border, measure the quilt as in Step 1. Cut 2, 8-inch wide BLACK/BEIGE PLAID strips to this length. Sew the borders to the top and bottom of the quilt, and press.

Step 4 Measure the quilt as in Step 2. Cut 2, 8-inch wide BLACK/BEIGE PLAID strips to this length. Sew the borders to the sides of the quilt, and press. Stay-stitch a scant 1/4-inch from the raw edges to stabilize the quilt before the quilt is appliquéd.

Adding the Appliqué

Step 1 Position the fusible web over the appliqué patterns, paper side up. Trace 4 pattern A, 4 pattern B, and 16 pattern C, leaving 1/2-inch between each tracing. Cut out the pieces roughly 1/4-inch outside of the traced lines.

Step 2 Press the fusible web shapes onto the back of the fabrics used for the appliqués; let the fabric cool. Cut out the shapes on the drawn lines. Peel off paper backing.

Step 3 Position the appliqué shapes on the quilt. With a hot, dry iron, press in place. With 3 strands of black floss, appliqué the shapes using a buttonhole stitch.

Attaching the Outer Border

Step 1 Measure the quilt as you did for the middle border. Cut 2, 5-1/2-inch wide BLACK strips to this length. Sew the borders to the top and bottom of the quilt, and press.

Step 2 Measure the quilt from top to bottom, not including the borders just added. Add 1/2-inch for seam allowances. Cut 2, 5-1/2-inch wide BLACK strips to this length. Sew 5-1/2-inch GOLD corner squares to both ends of the border strips. Sew the borders to the sides of the quilt, and press.

Putting It All Together

Step 1 Trim the backing and batting so they are 4-inches larger than the quilt top.

Step 2 Mark the quilt top for quilting. Layer the backing, batting, and quilt top. Baste the 3 layers together and quilt.

Step 3 When quilting is complete, hand-baste the 3 layers together a scant 1/4-inch from the edge. This hand basting keeps the layers from shifting and prevents puckers from forming when adding the binding. Trim excess batting and backing even with the edge of the quilt top.

Binding

Cutting

From RED PRINT:
- Cut 4, 2-3/4 x 42-inch strips.

Step 1 Diagonally piece the strips together. Fold the strips in half lengthwise, wrong sides together, and press.

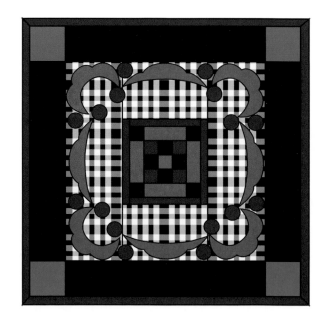

Step 2 With raw edges of the binding and quilt top even, stitch with a 3/8-inch seam allowance.

Step 3 Miter binding at the corners. To do so, stop sewing 3/8-inch from the corner of the quilt. Flip the binding strip up and away from the quilt, then fold the binding

down even with the raw edge of the quilt. Begin sewing at the upper edge. Miter all 4 corners in this manner.

Step 4 Bring the folded edge of the binding to the back of the quilt and hand sew the binding in place.

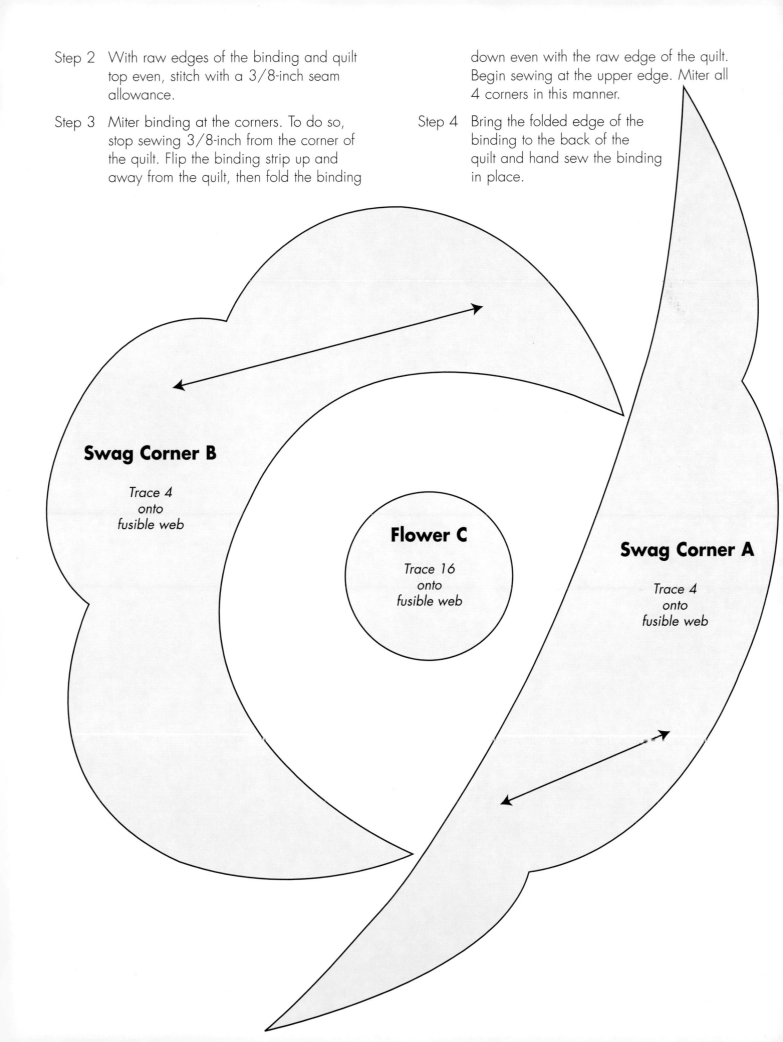

Swag Corner B

*Trace 4
onto
fusible web*

Flower C

*Trace 16
onto
fusible web*

Swag Corner A

*Trace 4
onto
fusible web*

SMALL BUT SPIRITED

For a small guest room Lynette chooses a Christmas red and country blue decorating theme focused on scaling everything down to make the room seem a bit larger.

In the bedroom shown here, a single bed boasts a tin ceiling panel insert framed by the wreath-topped headboard.

The small-scale bedside table features a tiny tree nestled in a blue spatterware dish pan. The wax Santa boots, chenille garland and miniature candy canes are all antiques from Lynette's collection. The plastic reindeer ornament collection on the tree was started by a favorite tree ornament Lynette had as a child. In the child's chair, a stuffed teddy bear holds one of two tiny pillows with quick appliqués that Lynette designed to be paired for bigger impact.

For a final touch of whimsy, grazing on a bed of greens on the dresser, Lynette displays a vintage 1950 Rudolph the Red Nosed Reindeer night light with music box.

SNOWMAN AND STAR PILLOWS

Fabrics and Supplies (for one pillow)

- 8-inch square of fabric for small star (cotton, flannel, or wool)
- 9-inch square of fabric for large star (cotton, flannel, or wool)
- 5-inch square of fabric for appliqué (snowman or house)
- scrap of fabric for house windows
- 9-1/2-inch square black solid for pillow top
- 9-1/2-inch square print for pillow back
- #8 black Perle cotton for all appliqués
- #8 gold Perle cotton for snowman nose
- 1/2 yard paper-backed fusible web for the appliqués
- polyester fiberfill to stuff pillow

Pillow Top

Cutting (from the fusible web)
- Cut one 9-inch square for large star.
- Cut one 8-inch square for small star.
- Cut one 5-inch square for appliqué.

Fusible web appliqué

Two small pillows are sometimes better than one. Here, a double-star is the background for a simple house or snowman appliqué motif. I make them in multiples for bedroom accents or quick gifts.

Step 1   Trace the small star onto the paper side of the 8-inch square of fusible web. Cut around the shape, leaving a small margin beyond the drawn line.

Step 2   Following the manufacturer's instructions, apply the small star fusible web shape to the wrong side of the selected fabric. Let cool and cut on the drawn line. Remove the paper backing.

Step 3   Fuse the star to the 9-inch square of fabric being used for the large star.

Step 4   Using black Perle cotton, buttonhole-stitch around the small star.

Step 5   Choose an appliqué shape and trace it on the paper side of the 5-inch square of

fusible web. Cut around the shape, leaving a small margin beyond the drawn line.

Step 6   Following the manufacturer's instructions, apply the fusible web shape to the wrong side of the selected fabric. Let cool and cut out on the drawn line. Remove the paper backing.

Step 7   Position the appliqué shape on the star unit and fuse in place. Using black Perle cotton, buttonhole-stitch around the shape. *Note: The snowman's features are straight stitched.* Use gold Perle cotton for the nose.

Step 8   Apply the 9-inch square of fusible web to the back of the Step 7 star/appliqué unit. Let cool and remove the paper backing. Trim away the large star fabric, leaving a 1/2-inch edge showing.

Step 9 Position the star/appliqué unit on the 9-1/2-inch square of black solid fabric; fuse in place. Using black Perle cotton, buttonhole-stitch around the large star.

Finishing the Pillow

With right sides together, stitch the appliquéd pillow top and back together, leaving a 3-inch opening for turning. Turn the pillow right side out and stuff with polyester fiberfill. Hand-stitch the opening closed.

House

Trace onto fusible web

Snowman

Trace onto fusible web

Small Star

Trace onto fusible web

PRETTY IN PINK

Even though Kerry is all grown up and recently married, her room, which has always been decorated in the softest of pinks and aqua hasn't changed a bit. Every year at Christmastime Lynette quickly transforms it into a pink-frosted pastel dreamland with the additon of just a few favorite accent pieces.

Taking center stage is a small tabletop tree laden with delicate glass balls in pinks, blues, and yellows. The recessed shelves next to the closet door are home to dozens of pastel pottery pieces.

Lynette simply fills all the flower pots with artificial snow, antique bottle brush trees, and more of the Shiny Bright ornaments from her collection.

The biggest transformation is the bed which becomes a twinkling night light with the addition of greens and lights to the headboard. Colorful pieced quilts and cozy flannel comforters layered together, along with a basket filled with candy canes in ceramic teapots and creamers, make the bedroom an inviting retreat!

NORTHWOODS NATURALS

Filling every nook and cranny is easy when the decorating theme is centered around the northwoods. Whether on shelves tucked into the eaves, or in storage partitions on the top of a desk, Lynette's collection of miniature bottle brush trees, houses, and cast iron animals brightens every corner of the bedroom.

Numerous quilts scattered about the room repeat the woodsy theme. Behind the four-poster bed, a simple tree fresh from the forest remains completely unadorned except for a light dusting of twinkling lights giving the bedroom a warm glow all evening.

PILLOW SACK

20-inches square

Fabrics and Supplies

Yardage is based on 42-inch wide fabric

- 1-1/8 yards GREEN/BLACK PRINT for outer pillowcase
- 5/8 yard RED PRINT for contrasting trim and ties
- 20-inch square purchased pillow in coordinating fabric for inner pillow

Cutting

From GREEN/BLACK PRINT:
- Cut 2, 19 x 40-1/2-inch rectangles for double-thick outer pillowcase

From RED PRINT:
- Cut 1, 9 x 40-1/2inch rectangle for trim
- Cut 4, 4-1/2 x 21-inch strips for ties

Assemble the Outer Pillowcase

Step 1 With wrong sides together, baste the 2, 19 x 40-1/2-inch GREEN/BLACK rectangles together with a scant 1/4-inch seam allowance to form a double-thick layer to be used for the outer pillowcase. The double thickness of the piece will make the pillowcase more stable.

Step 2 To make the ties, with right sides together, fold the 4-1/2 x 21-inch RED strips in half lengthwise. Stitch the long raw edges together, with a diagonal seam at one end. Trim the seam allowance to 1/4-inch at the angled end. Leave the other end of the tie unstitched. Turn the tie right side out, and press. Make a total of 4 ties.

Trim to 1/4"

Step 3 With raw edges even, position the ties on the 'outside' of the double-thick GREEN/BLACK rectangle. Baste the ties in place.

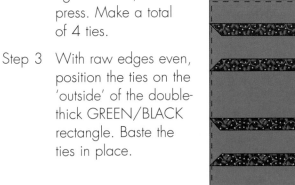

Step 4 With wrong sides together, fold the 9 x 40-1/2-inch RED rectangle in half length-wise, and press. With raw edges even, pin the folded trim to the inside of the double-thick GREEN/BLACK rectangle. Stitch in place with a 3/8-inch seam allowance.

Step 5 Fold the trim to the outside of the pillowcase, so that the folded edge of the trim just covers the stitching line, and edge stitch so 2-inches of the RED trim is showing.

Step 6 With right sides together, stitch the end and side of the pillowcase, using a 3/8-inch seam allowance. Turn the pillowcase right side out.

Step 7 Insert the purchsed 20-inch square inner pillow into the outer pillowcase, and tie each of the ties in a bow.

In the northwoods bedroom, pillows that stay on the bed year-round get all dressed up for Christmas in a hurry with a pillow sack and ties made stitched up from wintertime fun printed fabric Lynette designed for Thimbleberries.®

WINTER WARMERS

To fill a bedroom with soft comfort, Lynette is certain that you just can't have too many quilts. Keeping them within easy reach of a chair or the bed makes the room a welcoming retreat for family and holiday guests alike.

Here, quilts with patterns like "Winter Woods" (shown on the following page) are folded and stacked on a wicker ottoman in an alcove of the the winter woodland-themed bedroom.

In the same room, the top shelf of a bucket bench, opposite, displays vintage papier-mache' Santas, a forest of bottle brush trees, and snowmen. On the middle shelf, a carpenter's tool caddy holds greens, sugar pine cones, and berries celebrating nature's bounty. On the lower shelf, another tool caddy is home to even more quilts in forest green and deep red fabric color combinations that add to the feeling of a room filled with peace and rustic tranquility.

WINTER WOODS QUILT

Size: 48-inches square

Fabrics and Supplies

Yardage is based on 42-inch wide fabric

- 1/8 yard RED PRINT #1 for house
- 3/4 yard RED PRINT #2 for star points and outer border
- 1/8 yard RED PRINT #3 for lattice posts
- 5/8 yard GREEN PRINT #1 for outer roof section and trees
- 1/4 yard GREEN PRINT #2 for corner squares
- 1/2 yard GREEN FLORAL for star center and pinwheels
- 5/8 yard BROWN PRINT #1 for inner roof, door, shutters, and pinwheels
- 1/8 yard BROWN PRINT #2 for tree trunks
- 1/2 yard BLACK PRINT for lattice pieces
- 4 x 5-inch piece GOLD PRINT for window
- 1-1/4 yards BEIGE PRINT for background
- 5/8 yard BLACK PRINT for binding
- 3 yards backing fabric
- Quilt batting, at least 52-inches square
- A rotary cutter, mat, and wide clear plastic ruler with 1/8-inch markings

House Block

Cutting

From RED PRINT #1:
- Cut 2, 2-1/2 x 6-1/2-inch rectangles for house.
- Cut 1, 2-1/2 x 3-1/2-inch rectangle for house.
- Cut 1, 2-1/2 x 4-1/2-inch rectangle for house.
- Cut 1, 1-1/2 x 6-1/2-inch rectangle for house.
- Cut 1, 1-1/2 x 4-1/2-inch rectangle for house.

From GREEN PRINT #1:
- Cut 1, 6-7/8-inch square for outer roof section.

From BROWN PRINT #1:
- Cut 2, 4-7/8-inch squares for inner roof section.
- Cut 2, 1-1/2 x 3-1/2-inch rectangles for shutters.
- Cut 1, 3-1/2 x 4-1/2-inch rectangle for door.

The "Winter Woods" quilt folds nicely into thirds for easy draping over a bed rail, chair back, or large ottoman in the northwoods decorating theme. The house and star blocks are each paired with a twin-pines block for a change of scenery when the quilt is folded for display. (To see the entire quilt, turn to the quilt assembly diagram on page 121.)

From GOLD PRINT:
- Cut 1, 2-1/2 x 3-1/2-inch rectangle for window.

From BEIGE PRINT:
- Cut 1, 6-7/8 x 42-inch strip. From this strip cut 1, 6-7/8-inch square for roof background. Cut the star block background from the remainder of the strip.

Assembling the Roof Unit

Step 1 Layer the 6-7/8-inch BEIGE square and the 6-7/8-inch GREEN square. Cut the layered squares in half diagonally. Stitch 1/4-inch from the diagonal edge of each pair of triangles. Press the seam allowance toward the darker fabric.

Make 2

Step 2 Position the 4-7/8-inch BROWN squares on the corner of the GREEN triangles. Draw a diagonal line on the BROWN square; stitch on the line.

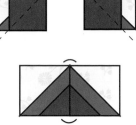

Trim the seam allowance to 1/4-inch. Press the seam allowance toward the BROWN fabric. Sew the 2 pieced squares together to form a roof unit which should measure 6-1/2 x 12-1/2-inches.

Assembling the House

Step 1 Sew the 2-1/2 x 3-1/2-inch RED rectangle to the 3-1/2 x 4-1/2-inch BROWN door rectangle, and press.

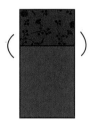

Step 2 Sew a 1-1/2 x 3-1/2-inch BROWN shutter rectangle to both sides of the 2-1/2 x 3-1/2-inch GOLD window rectangle. Press the seam allowances toward the darker fabric.

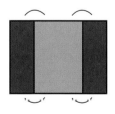

Step 3 Sew the 2-1/2 x 4-1/2-inch RED rectangle to the top of the window unit, and sew the 1-1/2 x 4-1/2-inch RED rectangle to the bottom.

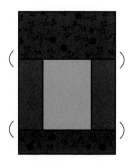

Step 4 Sew a 2-1/2 x 6-1/2-inch RED rectangle to both sides of the door unit, and press. Sew the 1-1/2 x 6-1/2-inch RED rectangle to the window unit, and press. Sew these 2 units together, and press. At this point the base unit should measure 6-1/2 x 12-1/2-inches.

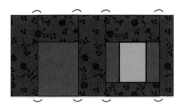

Step 5 Sew the roof and base units together to complete the house block. The house block should measure 12-1/2-inches square at this point.

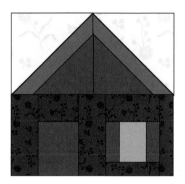

Star Block

Cutting

From RED PRINT #2:
- Cut 8, 3-1/2-inch squares.

From GREEN FLORAL:
- Cut 1, 6-1/2-inch square.

From BEIGE:
- Cut 4, 3-1/2 x 6-1/2-inch rectangles.
- Cut 4, 3-1/2-inch squares.

Assembling the Star Block

Step 1 Position a 3-1/2-inch RED square on the corner of a 3-1/2 x 6-1/2-inch BEIGE rectangle. Draw a diagonal line on the RED square and stitch on the line. Trim the seam allowance to 1/4-inch. Press the seam allowance toward the darker fabric.

Step 2   Repeat at the opposite corner
         of the BEIGE rectangle.

Make 4 Star Point Units

Step 3   Sew a star point unit to the top and bot-
         tom of the 6-1/2-inch GREEN FLORAL
         square, and press. Sew the 3-1/2-inch
         BEIGE squares to the ends of the 2
         remaining star point units, and press. Sew
         these units to the center unit, and press. At
         this point the star block should measure
         12-1/2-inches square.

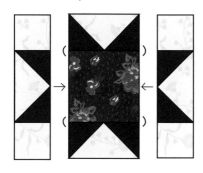

Tree Blocks

Make 2

Cutting

From GREEN PRINT #1:
- Cut 12, 2-1/2 x 6-1/2-inch rectangles.
- Cut 4, 3-1/2 x 6-1/2-inch rectangles.

From BROWN PRINT #2:
- Cut 1, 2-1/2 x 16-inch strip.

From BEIGE PRINT:
- Cut 2, 2-1/2 x 16-inch strips.
- Cut 8, 3-1/2-inch squares.
- Cut 24, 2-1/2-inch squares.

Assembling the Tree Blocks

Step 1   Position a 3-1/2-inch BEIGE square on the
         corner of a 3-1/2 x 6-1/2-inch GREEN
         rectangle. Draw a diagonal line on the
         BEIGE square and stitch on the line. Trim
         the seam allowance to 1/4-inch. Press the
         seam allowance toward the darker fabric.

Step 2   Repeat at the opposite corner of the
         GREEN rectangle.

Make 4 Tree Top Units

Step 3   Position a 2-1/2-inch BEIGE square on
         both corners of a 2-1/2 x 6-1/2-inch
         GREEN rectangle. Draw a diagonal line
         on the BEIGE squares and stitch on the
         lines. Trim the seam allowances to
         1/4-inch, and press.

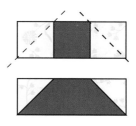

Make 12 Tree Units

Step 4   Sew a 2-1/2 x 16-inch BEIGE strip to
         both sides of a 2-1/2 x 16-inch BROWN
         strip, and press. Cut into segments.

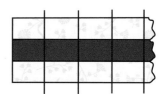

Crosscut 4, 3-1/2-inch wide trunk units

Step 5   Sew the tree units
         together. Add a
         trunk unit to the
         bottom and press.
         Make a total of 4
         trees. At this point
         the trees should
         measure 6-1/2 x
         12-1/2-inches.

Make 4 Trees

Step 6 Sew the trees together in pairs, and press. At this point the blocks should measure 12-1/2-inches square.

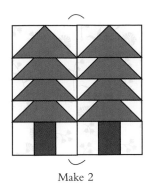

Make 2

Pinwheel Blocks

Make 10 from BROWN PRINT #1
Make 10 from GREEN FLORAL

Cutting

From BROWN PRINT #1:
• Cut 2, 3-7/8 x 42-inch strips.

From GREEN FLORAL:
• Cut 2, 3-7/8 x 42-inch strips.

From BEIGE PRINT:
• Cut 4, 3-7/8 x 42-inch strips.

Assembling the Pinwheel Blocks

Step 1 Layer the 3-7/8 x 42-inch BROWN strips and BEIGE strips together in pairs. Press together, but do not sew. Cut into squares.

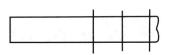

Cut 20, 3-7/8-inch layered squares

Step 2 Cut the layered squares in half diagonally. Stitch 1/4-inch from the diagonal edge and press.

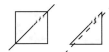

Make 40, 3-1/2-inch triangle-pieced squares
from BROWN PRINT #1

Step 3 Sew the triangle-pieced squares together in pairs, and press. Sew the pairs together to form 10 pinwheels. At this point the pinwheel blocks should measure 6-1/2-inches square.

Make 10

Step 4 Layer the 3-7/8 x 42-inch GREEN FLORAL strips and remaining BEIGE strips together in pairs. Press together, but do not sew. Cut into squares.

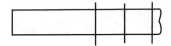

Cut 20, 3-7/8-inch layered squares

Step 5 Cut the layered squares in half diagonally. Stitch 1/4-inch from the diagonal edge of each pair of triangles, and press.

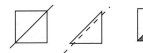

Make 40, 3-1/2-inch triangle-pieced squares
from GREEN FLORAL

Step 6 Sew the triangle-pieced squares together in pairs, and press. Sew the pairs together to form 10 pinwheels. At this point the pinwheel blocks should measure 6-1/2-inches square.

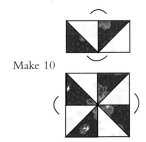

Make 10

Step 7 For the top and bottom borders, sew 3 BROWN pinwheels and 2 GREEN FLORAL pinwheels together, alternating colors, press, and set aside.

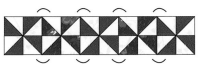

Make 2

Step 8 For the side borders, sew 3 GREEN FLORAL pinwheels and 2 BROWN pinwheels together, alternating colors, press, and set aside.

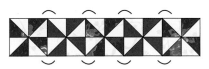

Make 2

Quilt Center

Cutting

From BLACK PRINT:

- Cut 12, 2-1/2 x 12-1/2-inch lattice strips.

From RED PRINT #3:

- Cut 9, 2-1/2-inch squares for lattice posts.

Assembling the Lattice Strips

Step 1   Referring to the Quilt Assembly Diagram for placement, sew a tree block and a star block to both sides of a 2-1/2 x 12-1/2-inch BLACK lattice strip. Sew a lattice strip to both sides of this unit, and press. Sew a house block and a tree block to both sides of a 2-1/2 x 12-1/2-inch BLACK lattice strip and press. Sew a lattice strip to both sides of this unit, and press. Press the seam allowances toward the lattice strips.

Step 2   Sew 2, 2-1/2 x 12-1/2-inch BLACK lattice strips and 3, 2-1/2-inch RED lattice posts together in a row. Make 3 lattice strips. Press the seam allowances toward the lattice strips.

Make 3

Step 3   Sew the lattice strips to the block rows. Press the seam allowances toward the lattice strips.

Borders

Note: The yardage given allows for the strips to be cut on the crosswise grain. Diagonally piece the strips as needed.

From GREEN PRINT #2:

- Cut 4, 6-1/2-inch corner squares.

From RED PRINT #2:

- Cut 5, 3-1/2 x 42-inch outer border strips.

Attaching the Borders

Step 1   Sew the pinwheel borders from Step 7 to the top and bottom of the quilt. Press the seam allowances toward the lattice strips.

Step 2   Sew the 6-1/2 -inch GREEN corner squares to both ends of the pinwheel borders from Step 8. Press the seam allowances toward the corner squares. Sew the borders to the sides of the quilt. Press the seam allowances toward the lattice strips.

Step 3   For the outer border, measure the quilt from left to right, through the middle, to determine the length of the top and bottom borders. Cut 2, 3-1/2-inch wide RED strips to this length. Sew the borders to the top and bottom of the quilt, and press.

Step 4   Measure the quilt from top to bottom, through the center, to determine the length of the side borders. Cut 2, 3-1/2-inch wide RED strips to this length. Sew the borders to the sides of the quilt, and press.

Putting It All Together

Step 1   Cut the 3 yard length of backing fabric in half crosswise to make 2, 1-1/2 yard lengths. Remove the selvages and sew the 2 lengths together, and press. Trim the backing and batting so they are 4-inches larger than the quilt top.

Step 2   Mark the quilt top for quilting. Layer the backing, batting, and quilt top. Baste the 3 layers together and quilt.

Step 3   When quilting is complete, hand-baste the 3 layers together a scant 1/4-inch from the edge. This hand basting keeps the layers from shifting and prevents puckers from forming when adding the binding.

Trim excess batting and backing even with the edge of the quilt top.

Binding

Cutting

From BLACK PRINT:

- Cut 6, 2-3/4 x 42-inch strips.

Step 1   Diagonally piece the strips together. Fold the strips in half lengthwise, wrong sides together, and press.

Step 2   With raw edges of the binding and quilt top even, stitch with a 3/8-inch seam allowance.

Step 3   Miter binding at the corners. To do so, stop sewing 3/8-inch from the corner of the quilt. Flip the binding strip up and away from the quilt, then fold the binding down even with the raw edge of the quilt. Begin sewing at the upper edge. Miter all 4 corners in this manner.

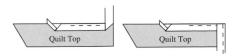

Step 4   Bring the folded edge of the binding to the back of the quilt and hand-sew the binding in place.

General Instructions

Getting Started

Hints and Helps for Pressing Strip Sets

Decorative Stitches

Diagonal Piecing

Metric Conversion Charts

Sources

GETTING STARTED

- Yardage is based on 42"-wide fabric.
- A rotary cutter, mat, and wide clear plastic ruler with 1/8" markings are needed tools in attaining accuracy. A 6" x 24" ruler is recommended.
- Read instructions thoroughly before beginning project.
- Prewash and press fabrics.
- Place right sides of fabric pieces together and use 1/4" seam allowances throughout unless otherwise specified.
- Seam allowances are included in the cutting sizes given. It is very important that accurate 1/4" seam allowances are used. It is wise to stitch a sample 1/4" seam allowance to check your machine's seam allowance accuracy.
- Press seam allowances toward the darker fabric and/or in the direction that will create the least bulk.

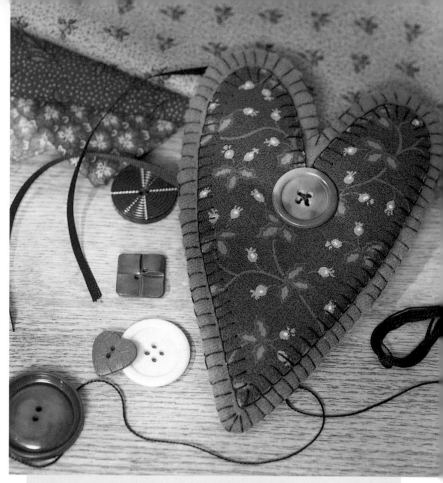

Nearly all the projects in this book are designed to be easy for you to make in plenty of time to relax and enjoy the holidays. I find that having all my supplies right at hand makes everything that much easier.

DECORATIVE STITCHES

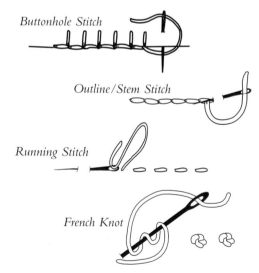

Buttonhole Stitch

Outline/Stem Stitch

Running Stitch

French Knot

HINTS AND HELPS FOR PRESSING STRIP SETS

When sewing strips of fabric together for strip sets, it is important to press the seam allowances nice and flat, usually to the dark fabric. Be careful not to stretch as you press, causing a "rainbow effect." This will affect the accuracy and shape of the pieces cut from the strip set. I like to press on

Avoid this rainbow effect

the wrong side first and with the strips perpendicular to the ironing board. Then I flip the piece over and press on the right side to prevent little pleats from forming at the seams. Laying the strip set lengthwise on the ironing board seems to encourage the rainbow effect, as shown in diagram.

DIAGONAL PIECING

Stitch diagonally

Trim to 1/4" seam allowance

Press seam open

METRIC CONVERSION CHARTS

cm—Centimetres
Inches to Centimetres

inches	cm	inches	cm	inches	cm	inches	cm	inches	cm
1/8	0.3	3	7.6	13	33.0	25	63.5	37	94.0
1/4	0.6	3 1/2	8.9	14	35.6	26	66.0	38	96.5
1/2	1.3	4	10.2	15	38.1	27	68.6	39	99.1
5/8	1.6	4 1/2	11.4	16	40.6	28	71.1	40	101.6
3/4	1.9	5	12.7	17	43.2	29	73.7	41	104.1
7/8	2.2	6	15.2	18	45.7	30	76.2	42	106.7
1	2.5	7	17.8	19	48.3	31	78.7	43	109.2
1 1/4	3.2	8	20.3	20	50.8	32	81.3	44	111.8
1 1/2	3.8	9	22.9	21	53.3	33	83.8	45	114.3
1 3/4	4.4	10	25.4	22	55.9	34	86.4	46	116.8
2	5.1	11	27.9	23	58.4	35	88.9	47	119.4
2 1/2	6.4	12	30.5	24	61.0	36	91.4	48	121.9

Yards to Metres

Yards	Metres	Yards	Metres	Yards	Metres	Yards	Metres	Yards	Metres
1/8	0.11	2 1/8	1.94	4 1/8	3.77	6 1/8	5.60	8 1/8	7.43
1/4	0.23	2 1/4	2.06	4 1/4	3.89	6 1/4	5.72	8 1/4	7.54
3/8	0.34	2 3/8	2.17	4 3/8	4.00	6 3/8	5.83	8 3/8	7.66
1/2	0.46	2 1/2	2.29	4 1/2	4.11	6 1/2	5.94	8 1/2	7.77
5/8	0.57	2 5/8	2.40	4 5/8	4.23	6 5/8	6.06	8 5/8	7.89
3/4	0.69	2 3/4	2.51	4 3/4	4.34	6 3/4	6.17	8 3/4	8.00
7/8	0.80	2 7/8	2.63	4 7/8	4.46	6 7/8	6.29	8 7/8	8.12
1	0.91	3	2.74	5	4.57	7	6.40	9	8.23
1 1/8	1.03	3 1/8	2.86	5 1/8	4.69	7 1/8	6.52	9 1/8	8.34
1 1/4	1.14	3 1/4	2.97	5 1/4	4.80	7 1/4	6.63	9 1/4	8.46
1 3/8	1.26	3 3/8	3.09	5 3/8	4.91	7 3/8	6.74	9 3/8	8.57
1 1/2	1.37	3 1/2	3.20	5 1/2	5.03	7 1/2	6.86	9 1/2	8.69
1 5/8	1.49	3 5/8	3.31	5 5/8	5.14	7 5/8	6.97	9 5/8	8.80
1 3/4	1.60	3 3/4	3.43	5 3/4	5.26	7 3/4	7.09	9 3/4	8.92
1 7/8	1.71	3 7/8	3.54	5 7/8	5.37	7 7/8	7.20	9 7/8	9.03
2	1.83	4	3.66	6	5.49	8	7.32	10	9.14

SOURCES

Many of Lynette Jensen's designs for quilts, pillows, and table runners shown in CLASSIC COUNTRY CHRISTMAS as decorative accessories are antiques from Lynette's personal collection, featured as projects, or available from her Thimbleberries® line of books and patterns or from Rodale Books. Please call 800/587-3944 to order a catalog or for more information on obtaining patterns for the projects sourced in the gallery below.

Starbound
(The Thimbleberries® Book of Quilts) — 24

My Stars (The Thimbleberries® Guide for Weekend Quilters) — 100

Prairie Pines (Single Pattern) — 34

Garden Path and Cottage Throw (Personal Collection) — 100

Cross Patch (North Bay Quilts) — 45

Starry Night (Mistletoe Mountain) — 101

Snowflake Tree Skirt (Single Pattern) — 46

Tall Houses (Single Pattern) — 106

Frosty Lights (Single Pattern) — 60

Log Cabin and Garden Pinwheel (Personal Collection) — 111

Scrap Patch Stocking (Single Pattern) — 60

Piece of Cake (The Thimbleberries® Guide for Weekend Quilters) — 112

Snowtopped Stocking (Single Pattern) — 60

Midnight Sky (Single Pattern) — 112

Seven Sisters (Personal Antique Collection) — 67

Pine Grove (The Thimbleberries® Book of Quilts) — 115

World Without End
(Personal Antique Collection) — 67

THIMBLEBERRIES®